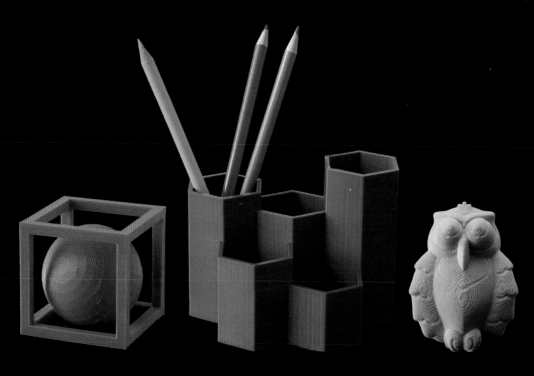

Penguin Random House

DK LONDON

Senior editor Ben Morgan **Assistant art editor** Sean Ross
US Senior editor Shannon Beatty
US Editor Karyn Gerhard
Jacket editor Claire Gell **Jacket designer** Surabhi Wadhwa
Jacket design development manager Sophia MTT
Producer, pre-production Andy Hilliard
Producer Nancy-Jane Maun
Managing editor Lisa Gillespie
Managing art editor Owen Peyton Jones
Publisher Andrew Macintyre
Associate publishing director Liz Wheeler
Art director Karen Self
Publishing director Jonathan Metcalf

DK DELHI

Project editor Priyanka Kharbanda
Project art editor Shreya Anand
Editorial team Vatsal Verma, Charvi Arora
Art editors Heena Sharma, Revati Anand
Jacket designers Suhita Dharamjit, Juhi Sheth
Jackets editorial coordinator Priyanka Sharma
Senior DTP designer Harish Aggarwal
DTP designers Vijay Kandwal, Sachin Gupta
Managing jackets editor Saloni Singh
Pre-production manager Balwant Singh
Production manager Pankaj Sharma
Managing editor Kingshuk Ghoshal
Managing art editor Govind Mittal

Photographer Dave King
Consultant James Floyd Kelly

First American Edition, 2017
Published in the United States by DK Publishing
345 Hudson Street, New York, New York 10014

A catalog record for this book is
available from the Library of Congress.
ISBN: 978-1-4654-6476-7

DK books are available at special discounts when purchased
in bulk for sales promotions, premiums, fund-raising, or educational
use. For details, contact: DK Publishing Special Markets,
345 Hudson Street, New York, New York 10014
SpecialSales@dk.com

Printed and bound in China

A WORLD OF IDEAS:
SEE ALL THERE IS TO KNOW

www.dk.com

3D PRINTING CONSULTANT
iMakr

Dorling Kindersley would like to thank iMakr for
their help in making this book. Based in London
and New York, iMakr is a leading provider of
desktop 3D printers, scanners, and design services
for 3D printing enthusiasts across the globe.

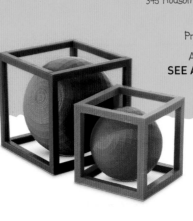

CONTENTS

 IMPORTANT NOTE TO PARENTS

The activities in this book may require adult help and supervision, depending on your child's age and ability. Always ensure that your child uses tools that are appropriate for their age, and offer help and supervision as necessary to keep them safe. The publisher cannot accept any liability for injury, loss, or damage to any property or user following suggestions in this book.

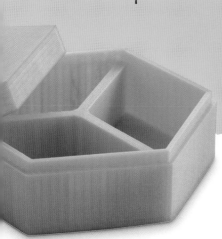

3D PRINTERS

3D printers are tools that let you turn the ideas in your head into objects you can hold in your hand. Instead of printing 2D images on paper, as inkjet and laser printers do, they create solid, 3D objects. They may look complicated, but once you understand the basics you'll see that 3D printers are surprisingly simple—as well as great fun—to use.

HOW 3D PRINTERS WORK

Most 3D printers create models with plastic. The plastic is fed into the machine as a thread, called filament, from a large coil. An electric heater melts the plastic, and the hot liquid flows out of a small nozzle, like ink out of a pen. As soon as the molten plastic is deposited, it cools and hardens. Computer-controlled motors move the nozzle back and forth, building up layers of plastic to create the model. Some printers only move the print head, but others also move the print bed—the base on which the model sits.

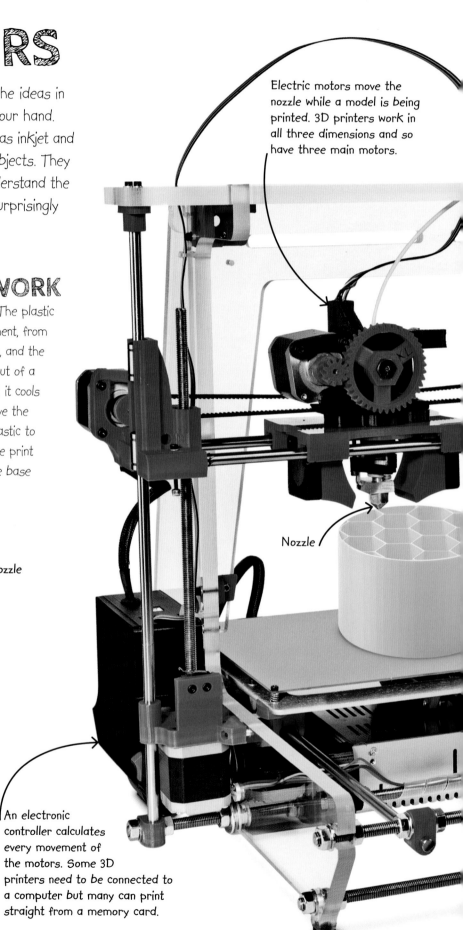

Electric motors move the nozzle while a model is being printed. 3D printers work in all three dimensions and so have three main motors.

Nozzle

An electronic controller calculates every movement of the motors. Some 3D printers need to be connected to a computer but many can print straight from a memory card.

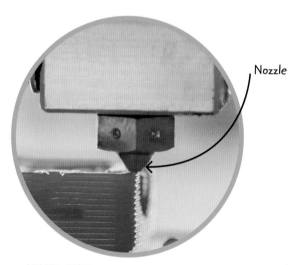

Nozzle

EXTRUDER

The most important part of a 3D printer is the extruder (print head). This includes the nozzle, the heater, and a motor to push filament through the nozzle. The nozzle "draws" with molten plastic, slowly creating a 3D object.

Filament being fed to the nozzle.

Belts on this printer move the extruder left and right as it prints.

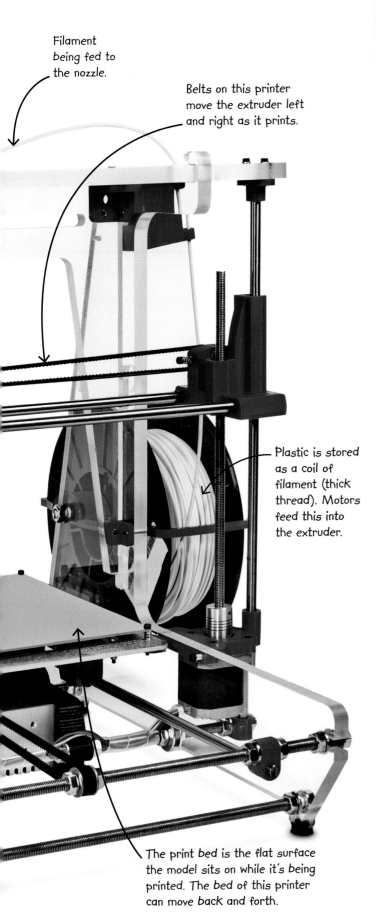

Plastic is stored as a coil of filament (thick thread). Motors feed this into the extruder.

The print bed is the flat surface the model sits on while it's being printed. The bed of this printer can move back and forth.

PRINTING MATERIALS

3D printers can create models from many different kinds of material, from plastic and metal to chocolate and even living human flesh.

PLA

The most popular material used in home printers is PLA (polylactic acid), a biodegradable plastic made from corn starch. PLA is safe to use and comes in many different colors.

PLA frog

RESIN

Some professional 3D printers use a smooth, translucent material called a light-activated resin. Resin printers use laser light to make the liquid resin harden into a solid.

Resin goblin

SANDSTONE

This stone-like material is made from a mineral called gypsum, which is mixed with glue and colored inks. It's used to print full-color 3D prints of scanned objects, including people and animals, creating miniature, lifelike replicas.

Sandstone dog

LAYER BY LAYER

Models printed in PLA grow from the bottom upward as the printer lays down layer after layer. The molten plastic emerges from the nozzle as a fine thread about 0.01 in (0.2 mm) wide, and hundreds of layers are needed to print large models.

3D MODELING

Many people who own 3D printers only print models they've downloaded, but it's much more fun to create your own models from scratch. This is easier than it sounds. To make a model, you need to use a 3D modeling program. There are lots to choose from, from complex professional CAD (computer-aided design) programs used by engineers and architects to simple online tools that anyone can pick up in minutes. Once you've mastered the basics, you can make anything you want.

This simple pen holder is made by joining five hexagons.

GEOMETRIC MODELING

There are two main types of 3D modeling program: geometric and organic. The next few pages show how geometric modeling programs work. To find out about organic modeling, turn to page 10. Geometric programs create objects from simple geometric shapes or lines. One of the best to use for this book is Autodesk® Tinkercad™, which runs in a browser window and works on PCs and Macs. Others include Microsoft® 3D Builder for Windows and Autodesk® AutoCAD® for students.

Desk caddy made in a geometric modeling program

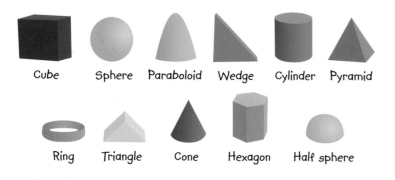

Cube	Sphere	Paraboloid	Wedge	Cylinder	Pyramid
Ring	Triangle	Cone	Hexagon	Half sphere	

WORKING WITH SHAPES

The simplest geometric modeling programs have a menu of ready-made shapes, or "primitives," like the ones shown here. Their names vary from one program to another, but they all work in the same way. Once you've chosen a shape, you can change it or combine it with other shapes to build more complex objects.

MOVING SHAPES

Before you can work with a shape, you need to place it on the "work plane"— a flat area that works like a table. In most programs, the work plane has a grid to help you judge distances in inches or millimeters. To move an object, drag it with your mouse—it will stay touching the work plane. You can also raise or lower objects by selecting them in certain places with your mouse.

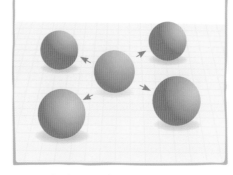

Moving an object horizontally

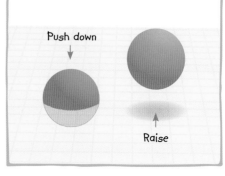

Push down

Raise

Moving an object vertically

COMBINING SHAPES

By combining shapes you can build almost anything. In many programs, when you push two shapes together they will remain independent, meaning they can be moved and resized separately. To make them into a single object, select both at once and then choose "group." Once grouped, they act as a single object.

Two different shapes

When shapes combine, the boundary line between them vanishes.

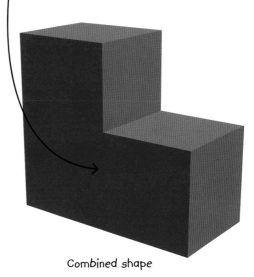

Combined shape

ROTATING SHAPES

When you rotate an object, it pivots around an imaginary line called an axis, a bit like a door pivoting at its hinges. In a 3D modeling program, you can choose one of three axes, called x, y, and z. The pictures below show what happens when you rotate an object a quarter turn around each of these axes. An object usually rotates as though the axis runs right through its center.

3D AXES

The x-, y-, and z-axes work like the axes of a graph. They can be used to pinpoint any object in a 3D space.

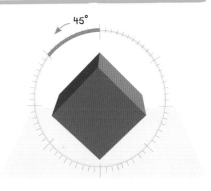

ROTATION TOOL

In many 3D programs, a tool like a protractor appears when you start rotating. Use this to set the exact angle of rotation.

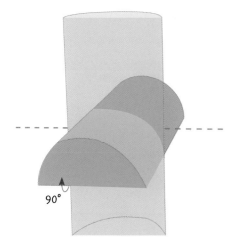

Rotating around the x-axis

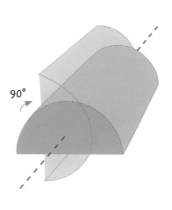

Rotating around the y-axis

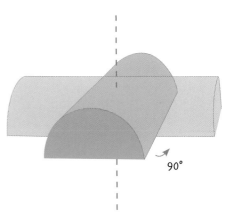

Rotating around the z-axis

RESIZING SHAPES

To change an object's size, first click on it to reveal its anchor points. Then click and drag an anchor point to stretch or squash the shape in any direction. Holding shift on your keyboard while you resize a shape will make it grow or shrink uniformly, without stretching unevenly in one direction.

Pull here to make the shape taller.

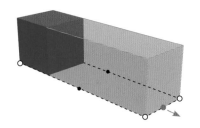

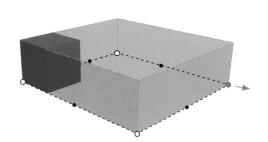

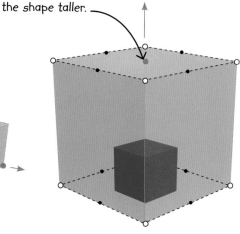

Pulling a central anchor point makes a shape wider or longer.

Pulling a corner anchor makes the shape both wider and longer.

Holding shift while pulling an anchor point changes the shape uniformly.

ALIGNING SHAPES

It's often handy to make separate shapes line up when you're modeling. 3D programs usually include an align tool to help you do this. You can align shapes by their centers or by any side, and you can do it in all three dimensions.

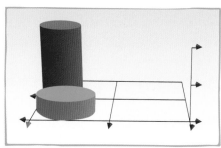

Shapes aligned on left

Click here to align the shapes by their tops.

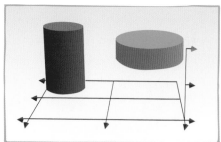

Shapes aligned by their tops

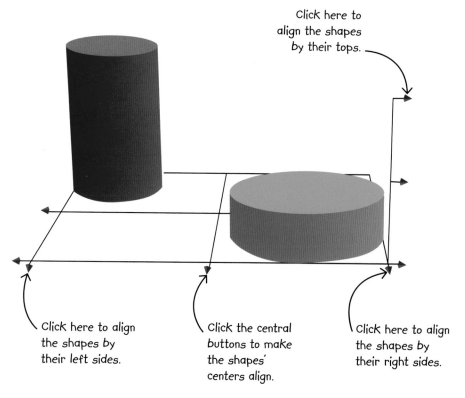

Click here to align the shapes by their left sides.

Click the central buttons to make the shapes' centers align.

Click here to align the shapes by their right sides.

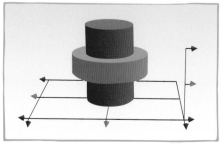

Centers brought together

MAKING HOLES

As well as adding shapes together, you can subtract one shape from another to create a hole. This is a very useful technique if you want to make parts that fit together, such as wheels and axles.

1 In your 3D modeling program, select two shapes, such as a box and an arch.

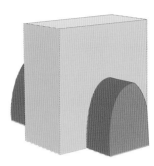

2 Merge the two shapes together. Most 3D programs allow you to slide one solid object right through another one.

3 Convert the part you want to remove into a hole. Depending on what program you're using, it may stay visible as a transparent object.

4 In some programs, such as Tinkercad, you need to group the objects to finish making the hole. The transparent object will vanish.

FROM 2D TO 3D

Most 3D programs have a limited range of basic shapes. However, many allow you to import 2D graphics and increase their thickness to make them 3D. This lets you create your own customized shapes—anything from cartoon characters and emoticons to your own drawings.

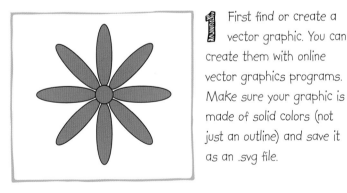

1 First find or create a vector graphic. You can create them with online vector graphics programs. Make sure your graphic is made of solid colors (not just an outline) and save it as an .svg file.

Bitmap graphic

Vector graphic

GRAPHIC FORMATS

2D graphics come in two main types: bitmap graphics, which are made of pixels, and vector graphics, which are made of geometric shapes. Check which type of graphic your 3D modeling program can import.

2 Import the .svg file into your 3D modeling program. Some programs automatically add depth, but in others you'll need to adjust the object's size.

ORGANIC MODELING

Objects in nature rarely have straight lines and square corners. Instead, they have complex, curved surfaces that are difficult to create in a geometric modeling program. To make such shapes, you need an organic modeling program. These programs use a mesh of interconnected triangles to simulate an object's surface. You can push and pull this mesh like a sculptor working a ball of clay to create any shape you want. The best organic program to use for the projects in this book is Sculptris™, but other good options are Meshmixer® and Blender®. Below are the main tools you'll find in an organic modeling program such as Sculptris.

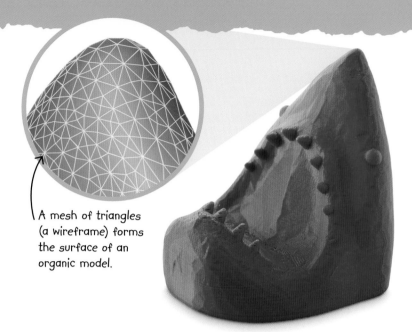

A mesh of triangles (a wireframe) forms the surface of an organic model.

Shark head created in an organic modeling program

GRAB

Use the grab tool to push and pull parts of your model in and out, creating rough shapes. Simply click the area you want to move and then drag your mouse to pull it. Adjust the size setting to control how much material you pull with the grab tool (shown in this book by yellow circles).

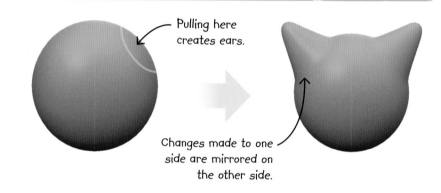

Pulling here creates ears.

Changes made to one side are mirrored on the other side.

INFLATE

Use the inflate tool to make an area swell outward. Overuse of this tool will make the area swell up like a balloon, so use it carefully. Inflate is handy for enlarging existing details, making them stand out more. As with the grab tool, you can adjust its size and strength.

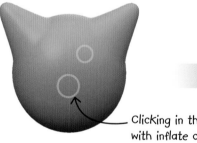
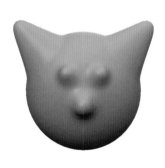

Clicking in the circles with inflate creates a nose and eyes.

DRAW

This is the best tool to use for creating fine details. When you drag it like a pen, it creates a ridge, adding more triangles to the mesh. If you set the draw tool to "invert," it makes a dip rather than a ridge.

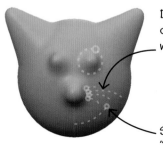
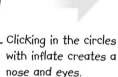

Draw here to create raised whiskers.

Setting draw to "invert" creates an indented line.

CREASE

The crease tool makes indented areas (dips) sharper and deeper. The longer you use it, the deeper the cut. If you want to sharpen a raised area, use the pinch tool instead.

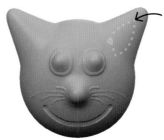

Using crease here makes a groove.

FLATTEN

To iron out bumps, dips, and creases, use the flatten tool with a small or medium size setting. To flatten out a large, rounded shape, use a higher size setting.

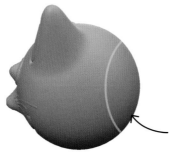

Click here to flatten the shape.

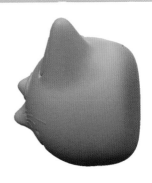

SMOOTH

This tool smooths out rough shapes without flattening an object's overall shape. Use it to give your model a more polished look. If you select a high strength setting when using smooth, you can use it like an eraser to get rid of details you don't want.

Use the smooth tool to soften the outlines around the ears.

SETTINGS

All organic modeling programs have a variety of settings that change the way the various tools work. Here are some of the most useful ones.

SYMMETRY

When symmetry is switched on, a change you make to one side of the model is mirrored on the other side. This makes it much easier to create human and animal faces and bodies, which are usually symmetrical.

STRENGTH

Increase the strength of a tool to make it work more quickly, with fewer clicks of your mouse.

SIZE

Use this setting to control the size of the area your tool affects. It works much like the brush size setting in a paint program.

INVERT

Switch on invert to make a tool have the opposite effect. Using invert with inflate, for instance, creates hollows.

DETAIL

When you increase detail, tools add new triangles to the mesh, making a model smoother and more detailed but increasing the file size. If you want to remove triangles to make the file size smaller, use the reduce tool.

SLICING

Once you've created a 3D model, you need to prepare it for printing by opening the file in a slicer program. A slicer works like an interpreter, translating the 3D data into a language your printer can understand. It converts the 3D geometry into a series of horizontal layers and calculates the exact path the printer's nozzle will follow as it lays down these layers. Slicers do various other important jobs too, such as adding supports.

A honeycomb pattern of hollows inside the model helps save filament.

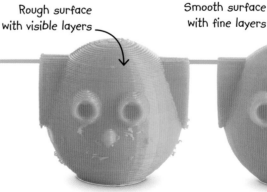

Troll model in slicer

USING A SLICER

When you open your file in a slicer program, you'll see the 3D model sitting on the print bed. Switch on supports to see if your slicer recommends adding them to stabilize the model while printing. To minimize supports, it might help to rotate the model or turn it upside down. Many slicers include a preview mode that shows how the printer will create the model layer by layer. Slicers also show how long the print will take and how much filament will be needed.

Supports prevent overhangs from sagging before they cool and harden.

Rafts and brims support the base and keep the model firmly attached to the print bed.

You can move the model anywhere on the print bed.

Troll model after printing

LAYER HEIGHT

Slicers include lots of useful settings that affect the quality and speed of prints. The layer height setting controls how thick each layer of plastic is. A small layer height results in a smoother model with finer detail but a longer print time. For a quick but rough print, choose a larger layer height.

Rough surface with visible layers

Smooth surface with fine layers

0.016 in (0.40 mm) layer height

0.005 in (0.12 mm) layer height

INFILL

To save filament and to speed up print time, slicers create a network of hollows and struts inside solid parts of a 3D model. You can control this by adjusting the infill level. An infill of about 15–20 percent is fine for most models, but for parts that need to be strong and rigid, choose a higher level. Some slicers also let you change the pattern of infill.

INFILL DENSITY

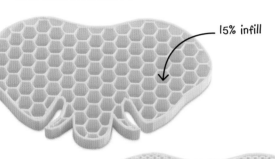

15% infill

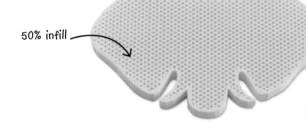

50% infill

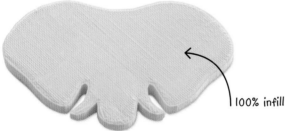

100% infill

INFILL PATTERNS

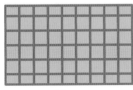

Linear

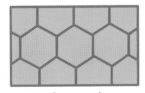

Hexagonal

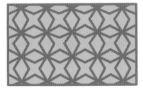

Moroccan star

Catfill

ADDING SUPPORTS

Parts of a model that overhang empty space can sag or collapse before the molten plastic hardens. To prevent this happening, slicer programs add supports. Slicers can also add rafts and brims to the base of a model. These help attach the model securely to the print bed and provide attachment points for supports.

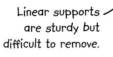

Linear supports

Linear supports are sturdy but difficult to remove.

Treelike supports look like branches and are easy to remove by hand.

Treelike supports

A brim is a supportive layer around the edge of the base.

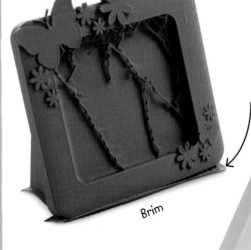

Brim

A raft is a supportive layer under the whole model.

Raft

AFTER PRINTING

Freshly printed models often need extra work to achieve a good finish. Any supports need to be removed, and rough edges might need to be filed down or sanded to make them smooth. Most 3D printers produce models in only one color at a time, but you can create multicolored objects by painting models or by gluing separate parts together.

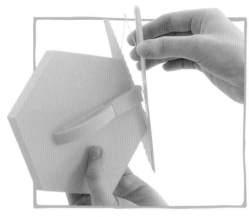

Removing a raft

REMOVING SUPPORTS

Rafts, brims, and slender supports are usually easy to pull away by hand, but some supports can be difficult to remove. Ask an adult to cut away difficult supports for you. If supports are too small to grip or hard to reach, use tweezers or small pliers. Supports can leave small scars where they tear off, so it's best to try and minimize their use by designing models that don't need them or by adjusting the settings in your slicer program.

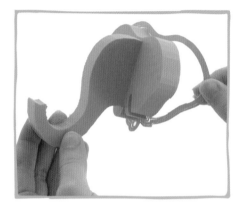

Removing a brim

Treelike supports are easy to pull off by hand.

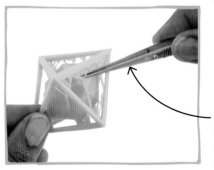

Use tweezers to grip the smallest supports.

SMOOTHING

If you want to make rough surfaces smoother, use a small file or some sandpaper. Take care not to damage fragile parts when you do this. Some 3D printing enthusiasts use chemical solvents to smooth the surface, but this doesn't work with PLA models and it requires special equipment.

PAINTING

To paint your model, use acrylic craft paint and a brush with a fine tip. You might find you need two coats of paint to get a solid color. To get a perfectly smooth finish, you can spray models with filler-primer to fill in tiny chips and grooves first. Ask an adult to do this for you.

Use a file to smooth rough surfaces

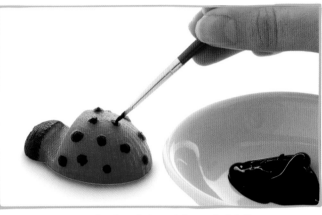
Use a fine brush to paint small details.

SAFETY BASICS

- When the printer is on, always assume it's too hot to touch. For maintenance or cleaning, unplug the printer and ask an adult to help

- Let a printed model cool down *before* pulling it off the print bed, and never touch a model while it's printing.

- If the extruder contains filament and isn't printing, don't let it heat up—it may burn the filament and clog the nozzle.

- Don't pull filament out of the spool or through the printer with force as it could damage the gears.

- Keep your fingers away from the extruder when your printer's motors are turning.

- Keep liquids away from your 3D printer. Liquid spilled on the electronics can cause serious damage and may even start a fire.

- Wear safety goggles when removing stubborn supports from prints— they will protect your eyes from flying fragments of plastic.

- Once the print job has started, don't open the printer's cover.

- If the printer nozzle gets blocked, turn off the printer and let the nozzle cool down. Ask an adult to investigate the problem.

Safety goggles

FIX IT!

Printing in hot plastic can sometimes produce surprises. Imperfections on the surface, a blob of extra plastic here and there, or even missing sections of a model can occasionally occur. Don't worry—there are easy fixes for most problems. Do remember to ask an adult to help too.

Warped base

Unwanted gap

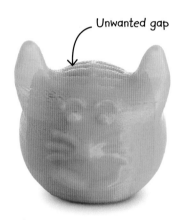

Twisted blob of melted plastic

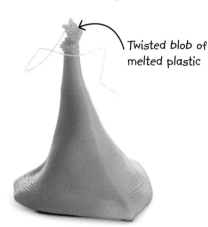

GAPS IN WALL

Your model may have unwanted gaps if it prints with very thin walls. Increasing the outer wall thickness in your slicer software will fix this problem.

TWISTED ENDS

If the molten filament cools too slowly, it may become deformed before it hardens. Use a fan to cool the filament or reduce the printing temperature and speed.

WARPING

If a model isn't firmly attached to the print bed, its base may warp (bend) as it cools and shrinks. To prevent warping, add a brim or improve adhesion to the print bed by covering it with painter's tape and glue.

You can often pull off areas of stringing by hand.

Uneven surface where supports were removed

Extra filament on top

Messy layers

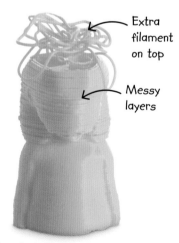

STRINGING

Stringing, or "hairy prints", happens when drips of plastic stretch into fine threads as the nozzle moves about. Reduce the printing temperature to avoid it.

AN UNEVEN SURFACE

If you use lots of supports on a model, it might have a rough surface when you remove them. The solution is to use the minimum number of supports.

MESSY LAYERS

These can occur if more filament than needed flows out of the nozzle. You can reduce the rate at which filament is fed into the printer to fix this problem.

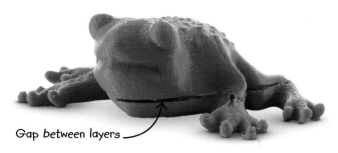

Gap between layers

MISSING LAYERS

If melted filament doesn't flow out of the nozzle quickly enough, you might notice unwanted gaps or missing layers in your model. Increase the feed rate of the filament to prevent this type of error.

SHIFTED LAYERS

If the print bed or nozzle is badly disturbed during the printing process, there may be an unwanted shift in the position of the remaining layers. Avoid fiddling with the printer when it is printing, or just start a fresh print.

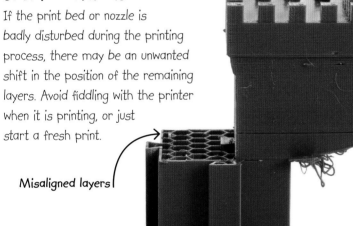

Misaligned layers

MORE PROBLEMS...

Here are a few more problems that you may have to troubleshoot. Seek the advice of an adult before taking any action.

◉ Clogged nozzle

Leftover dried filament from a previous print may stop new filament flowing freely from the nozzle. To fix this, clean the nozzle by heating it before you reload the filament.

◉ Elephant foot

This error causes the bottom of your print to bulge outward. It happens when the first layers haven't had time to cool and set before new layers pile up on top. Raising the nozzle height or cooling the print bed can help.

◉ Weak infill

Infill adds to the overall strength of your 3D print. If the infill appears to be weak or stringy, try alternative infill patterns and lower the print speed.

◉ Calibration

You may encounter all sorts of issues if your printer isn't calibrated, such as extremely messy prints. To fix, follow the calibration instructions that came with your printer.

EXPERT TIPS

◉ When printing objects with interlocking parts, you need to consider the tolerance, or space, around the parts that fit together. For a tight fit, keep a tolerance of 0.008 in (0.2 mm) on all sides. If you want a looser fit, make it 0.016 in (0.4 mm) on all sides..

◉ Any part of a model that overhangs the side at an angle of more than 45 degrees from vertical will need supports. When designing models, try to keep overhangs at angles of less than 45 degrees.

◉ Avoid delicate parts in your models. They may break off easily because they are fragile. They may even be too fine for the printer nozzle to print properly.

◉ Applying glue or painter's tape to the print bed before printing allows you to remove your printed model easily, especially if the print bed has become hot.

◉ Your 3D printer will need regular maintenance and repair to work efficiently. Get it serviced periodically.

DESK CADDY

Modeling and printing your own pen and pencil holder is a snap with this nifty project. It's the perfect addition to your desk, but it's also great for storing other odds and ends. You can print it in any color you like, and even personalize it with paint and stickers.

HOW TO CREATE A
DESK CADDY

This project uses a honeycomb arrangement of containers. The repeated hexagons join together to form a unit that prints in one step. You can alter the size and height of the hexagons if you want.

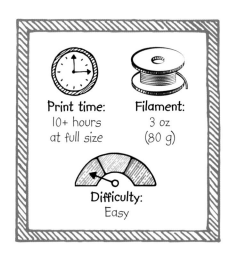

Print time:
10+ hours
at full size

Filament:
3 oz
(80 g)

Difficulty:
Easy

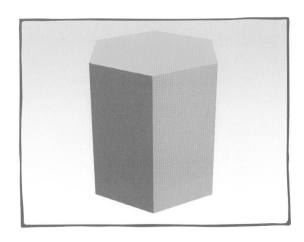

1 Start by taking a hexagon shape and placing it on the work plane. If your 3D modeling program doesn't include a hexagon, you could use a cube or a cylinder instead.

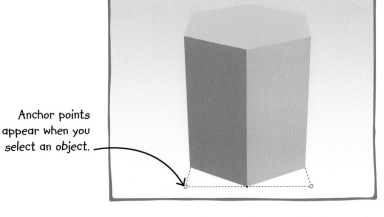

Anchor points appear when you select an object.

2 When you select an object, you'll notice small markers appear around it. These are called anchor points. You can use them to change the size and shape of an object.

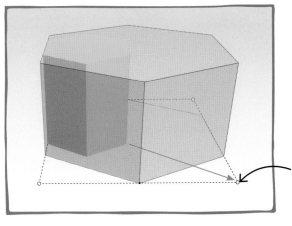

Pull an anchor point to enlarge the object.

3 Click an anchor point and try dragging it in any direction. The shape will stretch and squash as you move the anchor point around. We don't want this to happen, so click undo.

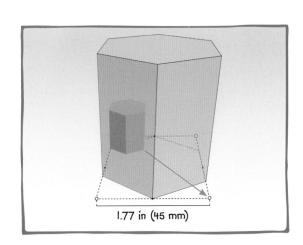

1.77 in (45 mm)

4 Now try again, but this time hold the shift key. When you hold shift, shapes change size uniformly instead of stretching. Holding shift, enlarge the hexagon until it's about 1.77 in (45 mm) wide.

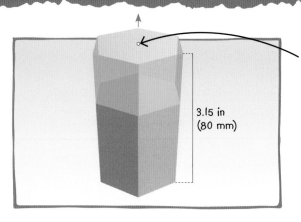

Pulling a central anchor point stretches a shape in one dimension only.

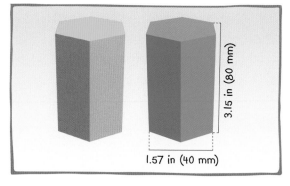

5 Next make the hexagon taller. Grab the anchor point in the middle of the top of the shape and pull it upward without holding shift. Aim for about 3.15 in (80 mm) tall. Again, the exact dimension doesn't matter.

6 Add a second hexagon (green, above). Repeat **steps 4** and **5**, but this time make the hexagon 1.57 in (40 mm) wide and 3.15 in (80 mm) tall.

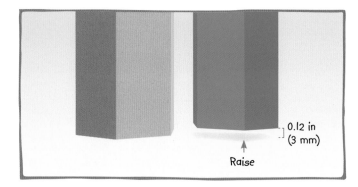

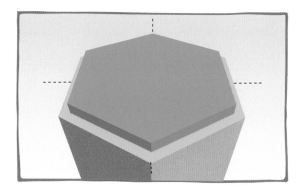

7 Raise the second hexagon so that its base is 0.12 in (3 mm) higher than the work plane. Take care to lift the whole shape, not just one face.

8 Select both hexagons and use the align tool in your 3D program (see page 8) to make their centers come together. Be careful not to move either hexagon vertically—the smaller one should remain higher than the larger one.

9 Select the inner hexagon and make it into a hole. If you're using Tinkercad, group the yellow hexagon with the hole. You should now have a hollow hexagon.

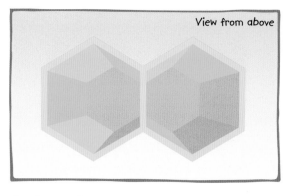

View from above

10 Make a copy of the hexagon and slide the copy sideways so one of its sides overlaps the side of the other hexagon perfectly. Hold shift when you move the shape. This stops it sliding diagonally across the work plane.

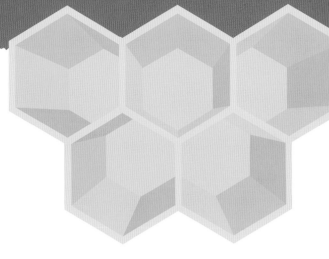

11 Make three more copies and arrange them in a honeycomb pattern. Your model is now complete and ready to be exported as a file that your slicer software can open (such as an .obj or .stl file).

NOW TRY THIS
You can adapt this model by changing the heights of some hexagons in **step 11** so all of them are a different height.

12 Open the file in your **slicer** program and set the infill at 15–25 percent to keep the model sturdy without using too much filament. This model has no overhangs, which means it won't need any supports.

13 This desk caddy takes about ten hours to print at full size, but you can speed up the print time by reducing the infill percent or by increasing the layer height at the slicing stage.

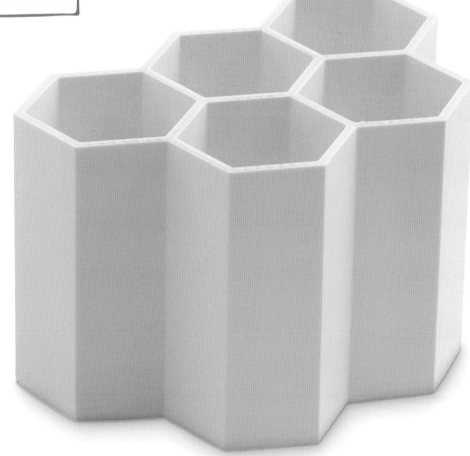

IMPOSSIBLE BOX

How can you trap a ball inside a box that's too small for it?
It might sound impossible, but you can easily create this
mind-bending object with a 3D printer. The trick is to print
them both at once, so the ball is trapped from the start.

You can use an
impossible box to
make a key ring.

HOW TO CREATE AN
IMPOSSIBLE BOX

In this project, you'll turn shapes into holes to make hollows in another shape. However, you'll also need to rotate shapes and align them. If you don't know how to rotate or align shapes, see pages 6–9.

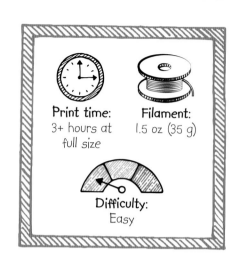

Print time:
3+ hours at full size

Filament:
1.5 oz (35 g)

Difficulty:
Easy

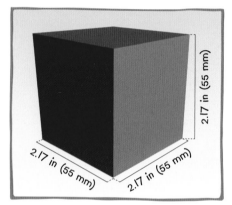

2.17 in (55 mm)
2.17 in (55 mm)
2.17 in (55 mm)

1 Start with a cube. Click on it and then select one of its anchor points. Enlarge the cube, holding shift, until it is 2.17 in (55 mm) wide on each side.

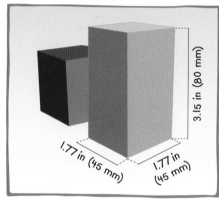

3.15 in (80 mm)
1.77 in (45 mm)
1.77 in (45 mm)

2 Add a second cube, shown here in orange, but this time make it 1.77 in (45 mm) wide on two sides and 3.15 in (80 mm) tall.

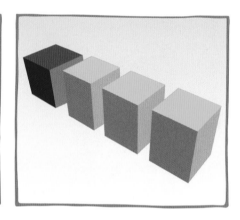

3 Make two copies of the longer box so you have one cube and three longer boxes in total. It doesn't matter where you put them.

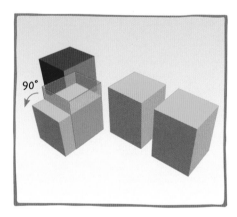

90°

4 Now rotate (see page 7) one of the longer boxes by a quarter turn (90 degrees) so it's lying on its long side.

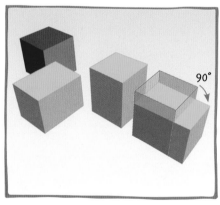

90°

5 Rotate another of the longer boxes by a quarter turn (90 degrees), but turn it to lie in a different direction.

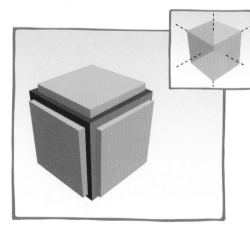

6 Select all four shapes and use the align tool to make their centers come together. Check that they match the picture here.

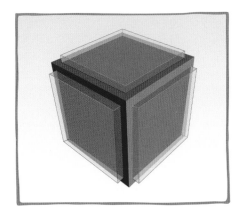

7 Carefully select the three longer boxes (but not the central cube) and turn them into holes.

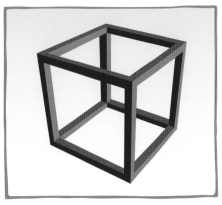

8 When you subtract the holes from the cube shape, you should end up with the **case** of your impossible box.

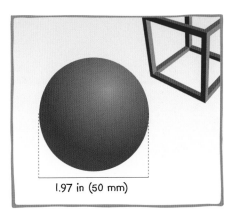

9 Now take a **sphere** and enlarge it, holding shift, until its diameter is 1.97 in (50 mm).

1.97 in (50 mm)

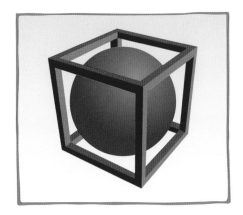

10 Place the sphere inside the box. Your impossible box is now complete!

11 This model will need supports. To print it with the minimum number of supports, rotate it by 45 degrees in your **slicer** program, and add supports and a raft.

12 After your printed model has cooled, carefully pull away the supports and the raft. If they won't come off, ask an adult to help you.

Pull the supports off the model.

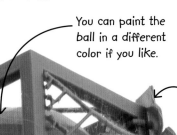

You can paint the ball in a different color if you like.

Raft

NOW TRY THIS
Experiment with more shapes, such as pyramids, cylinders, and hexagons, to create different combinations.

Ball in a hexagon

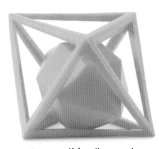

Impossible diamond

DINOSAUR STAMP

A personalized stamp allows you to print a picture, logo, or text in a flash. You can use it to sign letters and greeting cards or print your own wrapping paper. Making one with a 3D printer is easy—all you need is the imagination to think up your own design.

Hand-printed wrapping paper

Personalized envelopes

Gift tags

HOW TO CREATE A
DINOSAUR STAMP

This project shows how to turn a 2D picture into a 3D model to make a handy stamp or *badge*. You don't have to use a dinosaur—use any picture you like or just use text to create a personal name stamp. If you use a picture, you'll need to import it as a vector graphic. You can find out how to create vector graphics on page 9. If you use text, you'll need to flip it to make a mirror image so it prints the right way when you use the stamp.

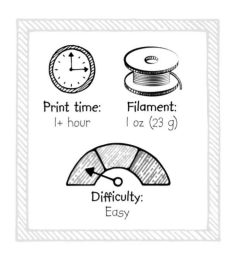

Print time:
1+ hour

Filament:
1 oz (23 g)

Difficulty:
Easy

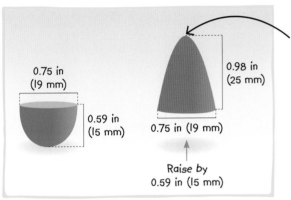

0.75 in
(19 mm)

0.59 in
(15 mm)

0.98 in
(25 mm)

0.75 in (19 mm)

Raise by
0.59 in (15 mm)

If your 3D program doesn't include a paraboloid, you can simply use a half sphere and stretch it.

1 To make a **handle** for the stamp, select a half sphere (green), turn it upside down, and change its size to match the figure above. Next take a paraboloid (red) and change its size too. Then raise it above the work plane.

2 Select the two shapes and use the align tool to center them in both horizontal directions (but don't center them vertically). Then group them into one shape. The handle of your stamp is now ready.

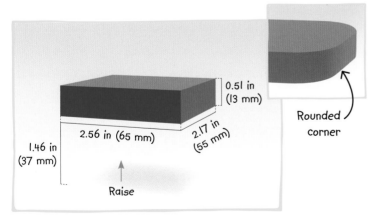

0.51 in
(13 mm)

2.56 in (65 mm)

2.17 in
(55 mm)

1.46 in
(37 mm)

Raise

Rounded corner

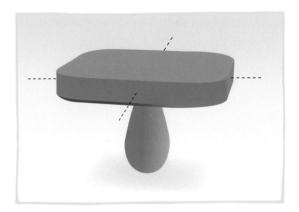

3 For the stamp's **base**, first resize a box to the dimensions shown, then raise it by 1.46 in (37 mm). Give it rounded corners if your 3D program has the option. To do this in Tinkercad, set the radius to 4.

4 Next, use the align tool to center the *base* and *handle* in both horizontal directions. Combine the base and handle into one shape. This is the **stamp**.

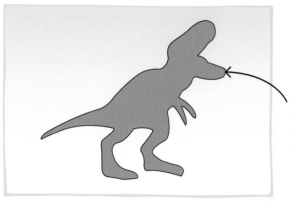

Make sure your vector graphic is a solid shape and not just an outline.

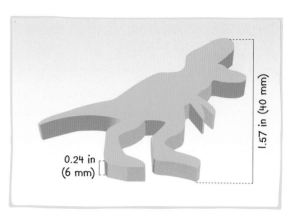

5 To create the stamp pattern, you need a vector graphic. You can create one yourself using an online vector graphics program, or you can use a search engine to find one. Save the graphic in a format your 3D program can import, such as an .svg file.

6 Open the vector shape in your 3D modeling program. While holding shift, change its length to about 1.57 in (40 mm). Then, without holding shift, make it 0.24 in (6 mm) tall.

0.24 in (6 mm)

1.57 in (40 mm)

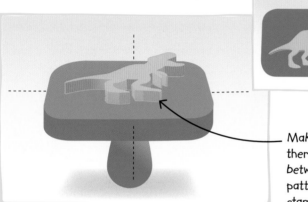

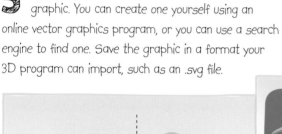

Make sure there's no gap between the 3D pattern and the stamp's base.

7 Place the pattern on the top of your stamp's base and embed slightly. Use the align tool to center the pattern horizontally on the stamp. Your stamp is now ready to be printed.

8 Open the model in your **slicer** program to prepare it for printing. You might find it prints best at a 45-degree angle. Add supports and a raft, as shown above. Set the infill to about 15 percent.

Press the stamp firmly onto the paper.

9 When the print has cooled and you've removed the support, try using it. Craft paint works better than ink. For a perfect print, use a paint brush to coat the stamp with paint before stamping the paper.

Create your own wrapping paper by repeating the pattern on a large sheet of paper.

NOW TRY THIS

Why not turn your 2D graphic into a badge? All you need to do is to add some small rings to hold a safety pin—just follow the steps below. You could also turn your graphic into a button by punching holes through it with your 3D program.

Dinosaur badge

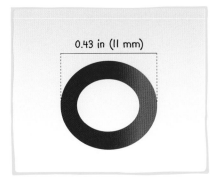

1 To create a **badge**, first place a ring on the work plane and resize it to 0.43 in (11 mm) wide.

0.43 in (11 mm)

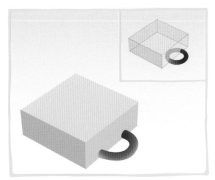

2 Make a box larger than the ring and place it so that it covers half the ring. Turn the box into a hole to slice the ring in half.

90°

3 Now rotate the half ring by a quarter turn (90 degrees), so that it stands upright on the work plane.

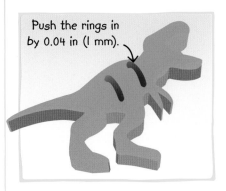

Push the rings in by 0.04 in (1 mm).

4 Import your vector graphic and make it 3D. Make a copy of the ring and place both half rings on the object. Check the distance between them to make sure your safety pin will fit.

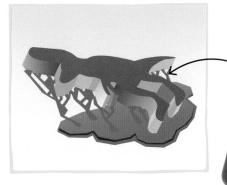

Supports

5 Open the model in your **slicer** program and add supports if your slicer recommends it. Set the infill to 15 percent and print your model.

6 Ask an adult to help you fit a safety pin under the rings. Then try fastening it to an item of clothing.

Keep the rings widely spaced so the badge won't wobble, but not so far apart that the pin won't close.

Add stick-on eyes to bring your coat hooks to life.

COAT HOOK

Why hang your coat on a boring metal hook when you can hang it on an elephant's trunk or a flamingo's neck? All it takes to make one of these quirky coat hooks is a bit of imagination. Once you've mastered the art of creating the animal shapes, you can print a whole zoo of animal coat hooks.

HOW TO CREATE A
COAT HOOK

Like the dinosaur stamp project, this project turns a 2D vector graphic into a 3D object that you can print. You'll need to learn how to create vector graphics to draw the animal's outlines. You'll also need strong adhesive strips to secure your coat hooks to a wall or door.

Print time: 2+ hours at full size

Filament: 2.5 oz (70 g)

Difficulty: Easy

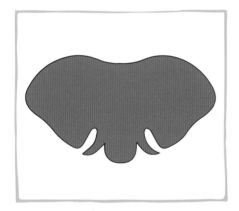

1 Use a vector graphics program to create the outline of an elephant's head seen from the front. See page 9 if you don't know how to create vector graphics.

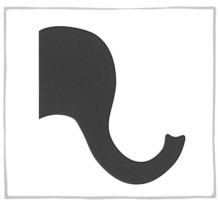

2 Create another graphic of an elephant's head from the side. The trunk will form your hook, so make sure it bends up at the end. Save the front and side views as separate files.

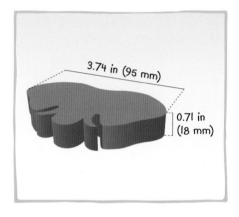

3.74 in (95 mm)

0.71 in (18 mm)

3 Import the first file into your 3D program. Hold shift to uniformly resize it to 3.74 in (95 mm) wide. Then, without holding shift, make it 0.71 in (18 mm) tall.

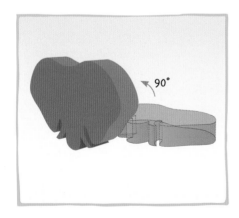

90°

4 Rotate the head by 90 degrees to make it stand on the work plane. If part of the head sinks below the work plane, raise it so it sits on the work plane.

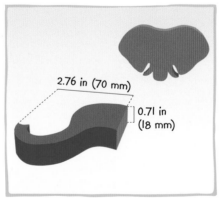

2.76 in (70 mm)

0.71 in (18 mm)

5 Import the trunk graphic into your 3D program. Hold shift and resize it to 2.76 in (70 mm) wide. Then make it 0.71 in (18 mm) tall.

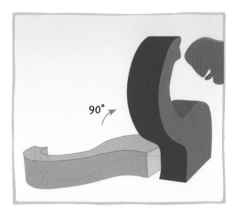

90°

6 Rotate the trunk by 90 degrees and make sure it's sitting on the work plane, as shown above.

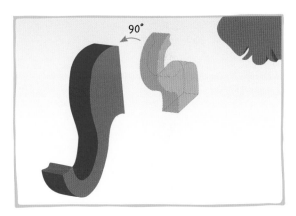

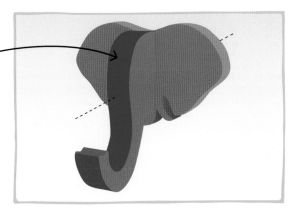

You can resize the trunk, holding shift, if it doesn't fit on the head.

7 Now rotate the trunk forward by 90 degrees so that the curve of the trunk touches the work plane.

8 Raise the elephant's head above the work plane and stick the trunk on it, making sure to align their centers horizontally. Your elephant hook is ready!

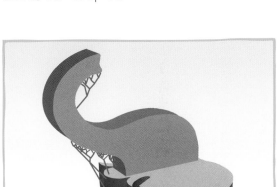

9 Open the model in your **slicer** program and rotate it so it lies on its ears, as shown here. The trunk needs supports to print properly. Set the infill to at least 25 percent to make the hook sturdy. If you expect to hang heavy coats on it, use a higher infill.

10 Use picture-hanging adhesive strips to fix your hook to a door, a wall, or a hook rack. Alternatively, ask an adult to drill holes in it so it can be screwed in place.

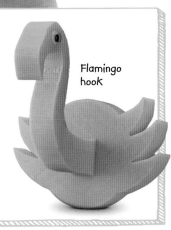

NOW TRY THIS

Give a shot at drawing other animal shapes and turning them into 3D hooks. Try a long-necked flamingo, a tentacled octopus, or a crocodile!

The head forms the octopus's back plate.

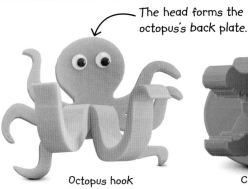

Octopus hook

Crocodile hook

Flamingo hook

PHOTO FRAME

Display your favorite pictures in this cute and colorful photo frame. You can also personalize it with your own drawings or name, which can be turned into 3D shapes and added to the design.

Create 3D decorations from drawings or graphics.

HOW TO CREATE A
PHOTO FRAME

Most picture frames have a removable panel at the back for adding photos, but this 3D printed version has a built-in slot that you simply drop photos into. The frame is designed for photos about 3.5 x 3 in (9 x 8 cm) in size, but you can change this by resizing it at **step 8**. Don't make it too big for your print bed though.

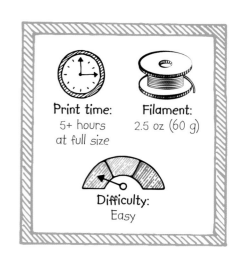

Print time:
5+ hours
at full size

Filament:
2.5 oz (60 g)

Difficulty:
Easy

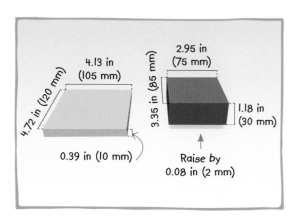

1 Start by placing two boxes on the work plane. Resize them to match the dimensions above. Then raise the smaller box by 0.08 in (2 mm).

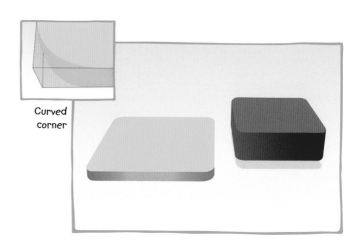

Curved corner

2 Make the edges round if it's possible in your 3D program. For instance, in Tinkercad this is done by setting the radius to 2.

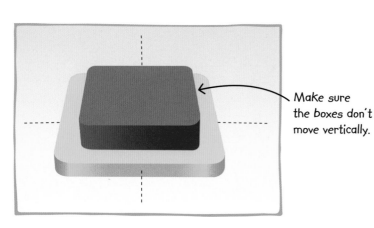

Make sure the boxes don't move vertically.

3 Select the two boxes and align their centers horizontally in both directions.

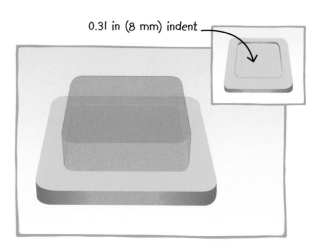

0.31 in (8 mm) indent

4 Turn the smaller box into a hole. You should now have a single box with a rectangular hollow.

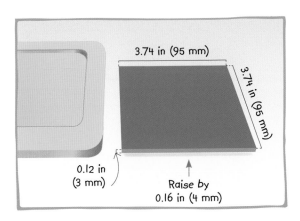

3.74 in (95 mm)

3.74 in (95 mm)

0.12 in
(3 mm)

Raise by
0.16 in (4 mm)

5 To make a **slot** for photographs, add another box and resize it to the dimensions given above. Then raise it by 0.16 in (4 mm).

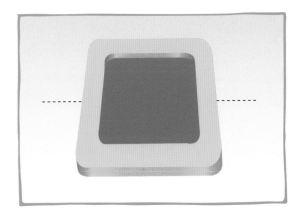

6 Use the align tool to center the two objects along the line shown above, without moving them vertically.

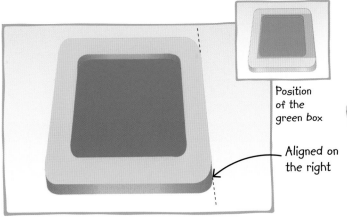

Position
of the
green box

Aligned on
the right

7 Now align both objects on the right.

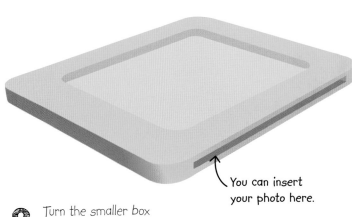

You can insert
your photo here.

8 Turn the smaller box into a hole. Your frame now has a slot.

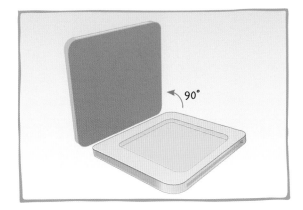

90°

9 Next, rotate the frame by 90 degrees to make it stand upright, with the slot facing upward. Make sure it's standing on the work plane.

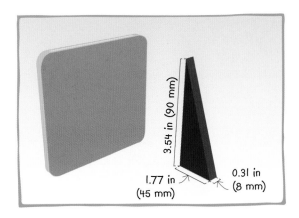

3.54 in (90 mm)

1.77 in
(45 mm)

0.31 in
(8 mm)

10 To create a support, select a wedge and place it on the work plane. Resize it to match the dimensions shown here.

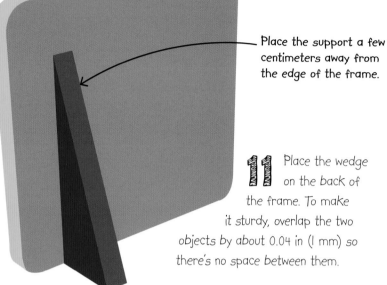

Place the support a few centimeters away from the edge of the frame.

11 Place the wedge on the back of the frame. To make it sturdy, overlap the two objects by about 0.04 in (1 mm) so there's no space between them.

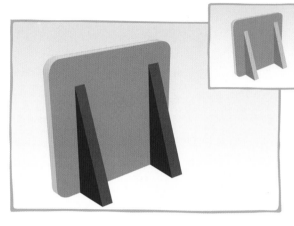

12 Duplicate the support and move the second one to the other end of the frame. Group all the shapes to make a single object.

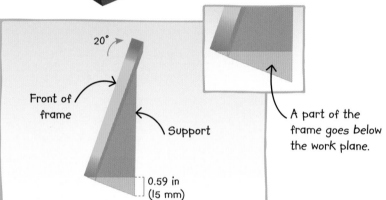

20°

Front of frame

Support

A part of the frame goes below the work plane.

0.59 in (15 mm)

13 Rotate the picture frame to the right by 20 degrees and then push it down so that its lowest point is about 0.59 in (15 mm) below the work plane.

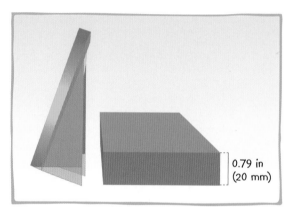

0.79 in (20 mm)

14 Place a cube on the work plane. Resize it to make it longer and wider than the photo frame, and about 0.79 in (20 mm) tall.

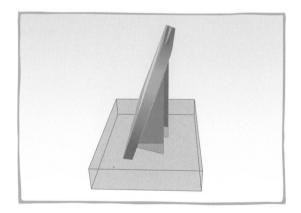

15 Move the box below the work plane and place it right under the picture frame. Turn the box into a hole to trim the parts of the photo frame under the work plane.

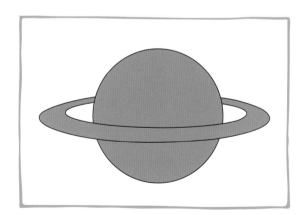

16 To create decorations, use a vector graphics program to draw any shapes you like (see page 9). Save the file in a format your 3D program can import, such as an .svg file.

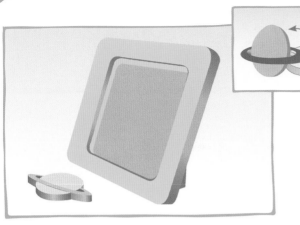

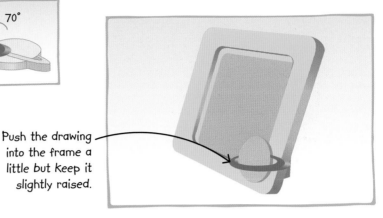

17 Open the vector drawing in your 3D program. Hold shift and resize it to your preferred size. Then rotate it by 70 degrees to match the angle of the frame.

Push the drawing into the frame a little but keep it slightly raised.

18 Place your drawing on one of the corners and push it into the frame slightly.

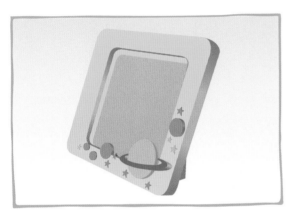

19 Repeat **steps 16–18** to add more decorations, or use your 3D program to add 3D text. Save your model.

Gently pull the supports away by hand.

Supports

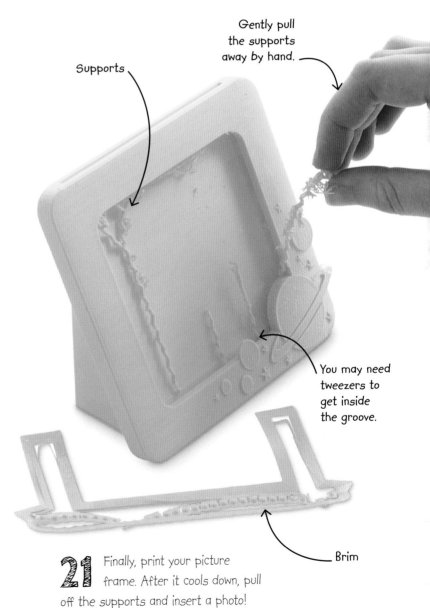

You may need tweezers to get inside the groove.

Brim

20 Open the model file in your **slicer** program. Add supports to the frame, as shown here, and add a brim to support the base.

21 Finally, print your picture frame. After it cools down, pull off the supports and insert a photo!

TREASURE BOX

This treasure box is perfect for storing all sorts of tiny keepsakes, from coins and marbles to gemstones and jewelry. It's very easy to adapt: you can make it in lots of different shapes, print the lid in your favorite color, or even add raised lettering or pictures to the surface.

Add dividers to make separate compartments.

The lid clips
tightly onto the
lip of the base.

HOW TO CREATE A
TREASURE BOX

The instructions here show how to make a hexagonal treasure box, but the steps are just the same if you want to make a round one or a square one. In some 3D programs, you can change how many faces a polygon has, which allows you to make a treasure box with any number of sides. Take extra care to follow the measurements exactly so the lid for your box isn't too tight or loose.

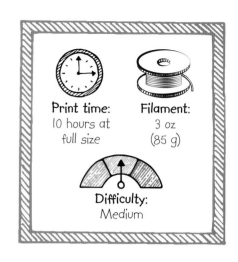

Print time:
10 hours at full size

Filament:
3 oz (85 g)

Difficulty:
Medium

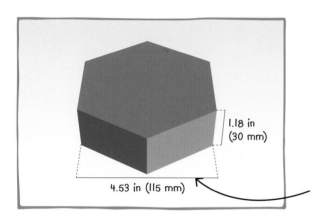

1.18 in (30 mm)

4.53 in (115 mm)

The width here is the distance from face to face, not corner to corner.

1 Start making the **base** of the box by placing a hexagon shape on the work plane. Resize it, holding shift, until it is 4.53 in (115 mm) wide. Then make it 1.18 in (30 mm) tall.

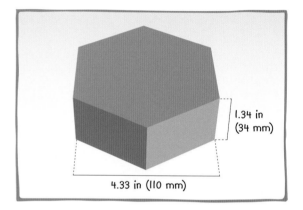

1.34 in (34 mm)

4.33 in (110 mm)

2 Add a second hexagon (red, above), but this time make it 4.33 in (110 mm) wide and 1.34 in (34 mm) tall.

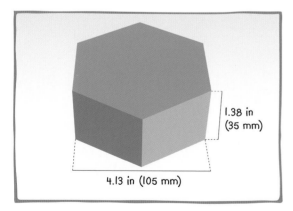

1.38 in (35 mm)

4.13 in (105 mm)

3 Place a third hexagon (green, above) on your work plane. Resize it to match the dimensions given here.

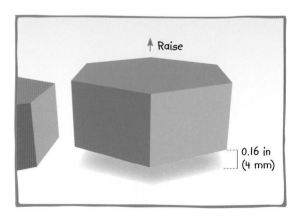

↑ Raise

0.16 in (4 mm)

4 Now raise the third hexagon so its base is 0.16 in (4 mm) above the work plane.

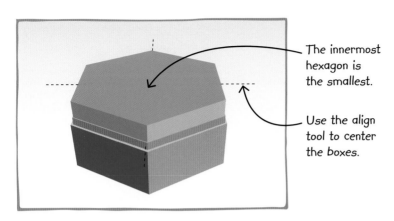

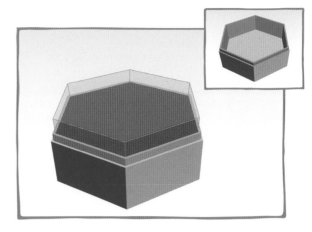

5 Select all three hexagons and align their centers horizontally but not vertically. The shapes should match the picture here.

The innermost hexagon is the smallest.

Use the align tool to center the boxes.

6 Pick the innermost hexagon and turn it into a hole. You should now have the base of your box, with a lip for the lid to fit neatly on top.

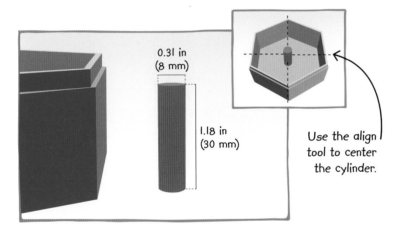

0.31 in (8 mm)

1.18 in (30 mm)

Use the align tool to center the cylinder.

7 Now take a cylinder and change its dimensions to a height of 1.18 in (30 mm) and a diameter of 0.31 in (8 mm). Place it inside the box. Using the align tool, make the cylinder sit at the center of the box.

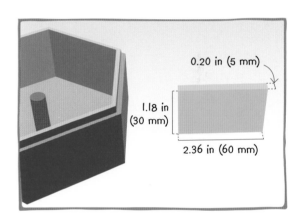

0.20 in (5 mm)

1.18 in (30 mm)

2.36 in (60 mm)

8 To create a partition, resize a cube to make a box 2.36 in (60 mm) long, 0.20 in (5 mm) wide, and 1.18 in (30 mm) tall.

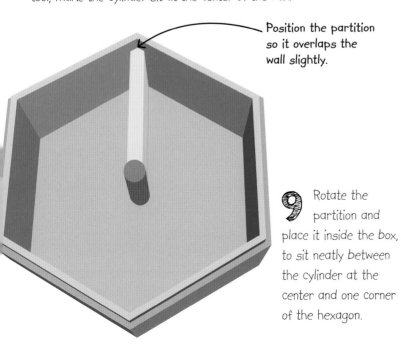

Position the partition so it overlaps the wall slightly.

9 Rotate the partition and place it inside the box, to sit neatly between the cylinder at the center and one corner of the hexagon.

120°   120°

10 Make a copy of the partition, rotate it by 120 degrees, and fit it in another corner. Then add a third partition and rotate it by 120 degrees in the other direction, so that your box has three compartments.

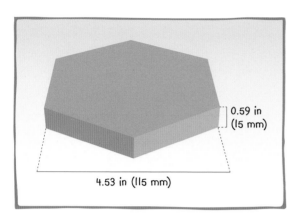

0.59 in (15 mm)

4.53 in (115 mm)

11 To create the **lid**, take a hexagon and make it 4.53 in (115 mm) wide and 0.59 in (15 mm) tall.

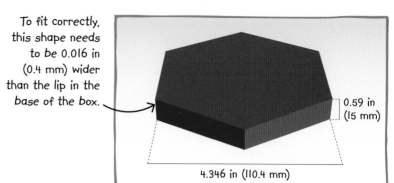

To fit correctly, this shape needs to be 0.016 in (0.4 mm) wider than the lip in the base of the box.

0.59 in (15 mm)

4.346 in (110.4 mm)

12 Place another hexagon on the work plane, but make this one 4.346 in (110.4 mm) wide and 0.59 in (15 mm) tall.

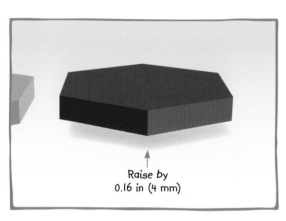

Raise by 0.16 in (4 mm)

13 Raise the second hexagon so its base is 0.16 in (4 mm) above the work plane.

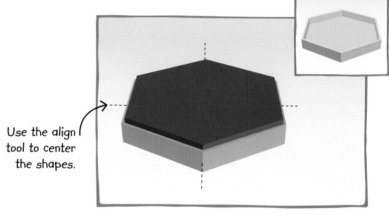

Use the align tool to center the shapes.

14 Select both hexagons and align their centers horizontally. Then convert the inner hexagon into a hole. You now have a lid for the box.

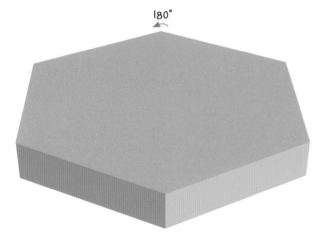

180°

15 Turn the lid upside down by rotating it 180 degrees.

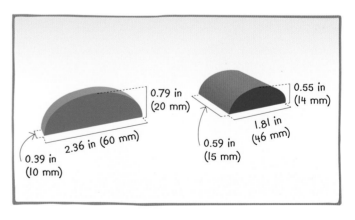

0.79 in (20 mm)

0.55 in (14 mm)

2.36 in (60 mm)

1.81 in (46 mm)

0.59 in (15 mm)

0.39 in (10 mm)

16 To create a **handle** for the lid, take two semicircular shapes and change their dimensions to match those shown.

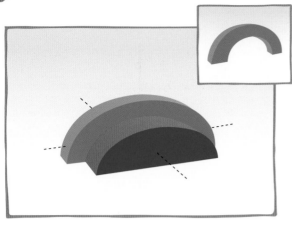

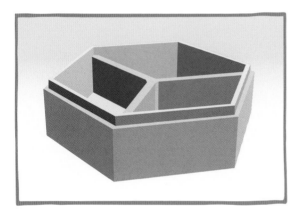

17 Align the centers of the two shapes horizontally. Make the inner one into a hole. You now have a handle.

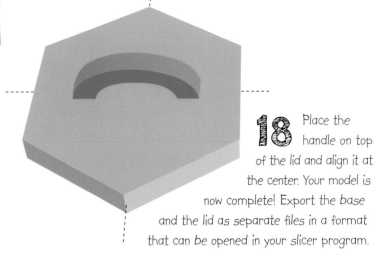

18 Place the handle on top of the lid and align it at the center. Your model is now complete! Export the *base* and the lid as separate files in a format that can be opened in your slicer program.

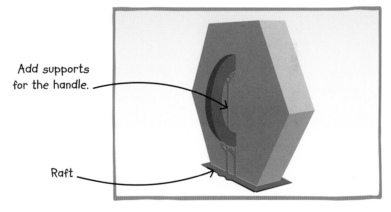

Add supports for the handle.

Raft

19 Open the *base* in your **slicer** program. As there are no overhangs, this structure won't need any supports. Set the infill to 15 percent and send it to your 3D printer.

20 Open the lid file. The lid is best printed vertically, with some supports for the handle and a raft under the *base*.

21 If you like, you can customize your box by printing the *base* and lid in different filament colors. You can also paint different patterns on the box.

PHONE STANDS

Phone stands are very handy if you want to watch a video without holding your phone. There are two designs in this project. The first is a pocket-sized phone stand that doubles as a key ring. The second is based on a shark's jaws and is big enough to hold a tablet computer.

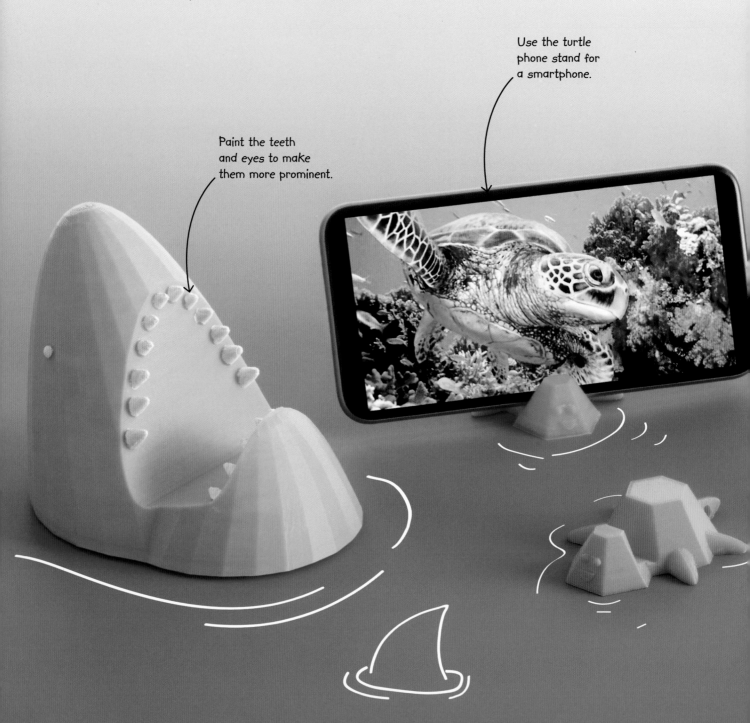

Use the turtle phone stand for a smartphone.

Paint the teeth and eyes to make them more prominent.

Use the shark stand to hold a tablet computer or phone.

HOW TO CREATE
PHONE STANDS

Follow the steps on pages 48–51 to make the turtle phone stand. Turn to page 52 to make the shark stand.

TURTLE KEY RING AND PHONE STAND

This phone stand is based on a turtle shape but you can adapt it into a dragon or a ladybird. You'll need to measure the thickness of your phone (including any case) to get the size of the slot right. Take care to get all the dimensions correct so you make a sturdy stand that won't fall over.

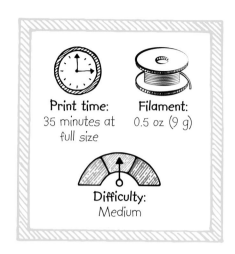

Print time: 35 minutes at full size

Filament: 0.5 oz (9 g)

Difficulty: Medium

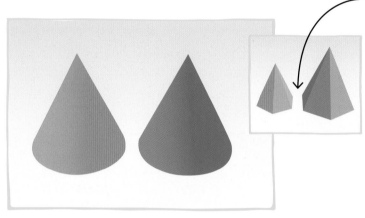

Make sure that sides face each other, not corners.

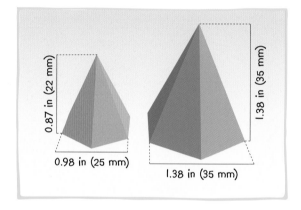

0.87 in (22 mm)

0.98 in (25 mm)

1.38 in (35 mm)

1.38 in (35 mm)

1 To make the **body**, place two cones on the work plane. If your 3D program lets you change how many sides shapes have, select both cones and give them six sides. If not, leave them as cones.

2 Hold shift and resize the first cone to a width of 0.98 in (25 mm) and the second one to a width of 1.38 in (35 mm). Now change their heights to the dimensions given above.

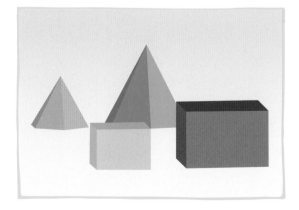

Each box should cover the top of a cone.

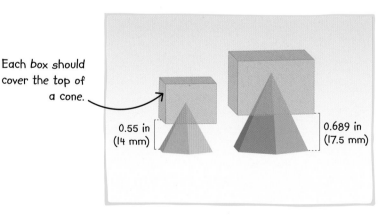

0.55 in (14 mm)

0.689 in (17.5 mm)

3 Add two boxes. Make the first box wider and longer than the first cone, and the second one wider and longer than the second cone. It doesn't matter if the boxes are taller than the cones.

4 Raise the boxes above the work plane, matching the heights shown here. Place each box on a cone, covering its tip. Turn both boxes into holes to trim the tops off the cones.

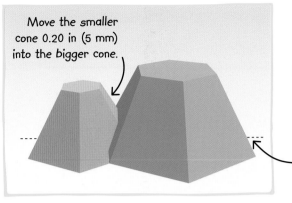

Move the smaller cone 0.20 in (5 mm) into the bigger cone.

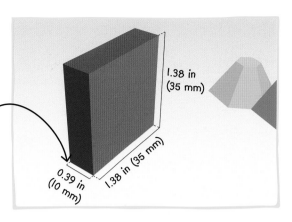

Adjust this figure until it's 0.08 in (2 mm) greater than the thickness of your phone.

1.38 in (35 mm)

0.39 in (10 mm)

1.38 in (35 mm)

Align the centers of the cones along the line shown here.

5 Move the small cone toward the large one until it touches. Then slide it a further 0.20 in (5 mm) into the large one so they overlap. Align their centers along the line shown above.

6 Place a box on the work plane and resize it to the dimensions shown above. Check how thick your phone is and make the box only slightly thicker.

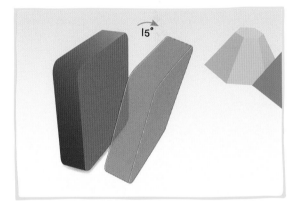

15°

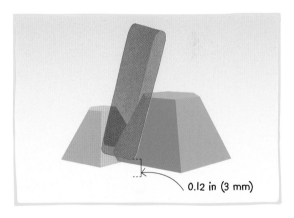

0.12 in (3 mm)

7 Make the sharp edges of the box rounder if your 3D program lets you. In Tinkercad, you do this by setting the radius to 2. Rotate the box to the right by exactly 15 degrees.

8 Now raise the box so that its lowest point is 0.12 in (3 mm) above the work plane. Place it in the area between the cones, and turn the box into a hole to create the **slot** for your phone.

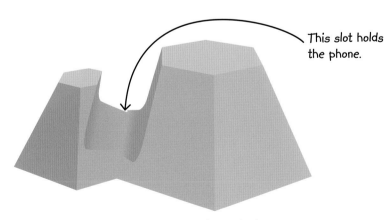

This slot holds the phone.

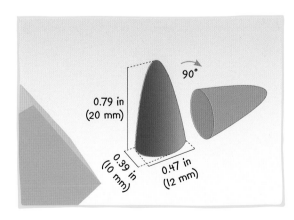

0.79 in (20 mm)

90°

0.39 in (10 mm)

0.47 in (12 mm)

9 Combine the two cones to make a single object. Your turtle phone stand is nearly ready. All that remains is to add some decorative touches.

10 To create a **tail**, take a paraboloid and resize it to match the dimensions given above. Rotate the shape by 90 degrees.

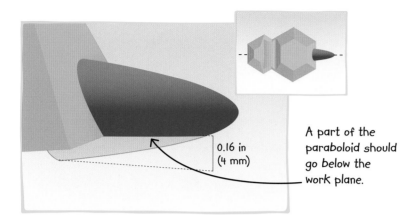

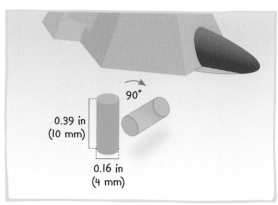

A part of the paraboloid should go below the work plane.

11 Place the paraboloid in the back of the turtle and push it down so its lowest point is 0.16 in (4 mm) below the work plane. Align along the center of the body.

12 Put a cylinder on the work plane. Resize it to a height of 0.39 in (10 mm) and a diameter of 0.16 in (4 mm). Rotate it by a quarter turn (90 degrees).

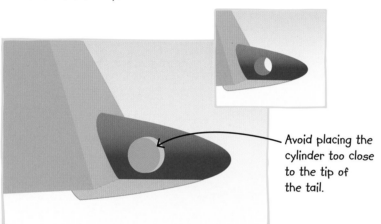

Avoid placing the cylinder too close to the tip of the tail.

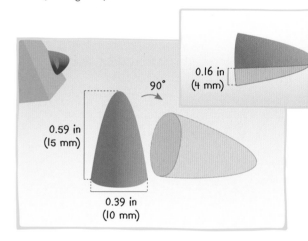

13 Put the cylinder inside the paraboloid, above the work plane, making sure it sticks out on both sides. Turn it into a hole. This will hold a key ring.

14 To create a **leg**, resize a paraboloid to the dimensions shown here and rotate it by 90 degrees. Push it down so that a part of it, as shown in the small picture, sits below the work plane.

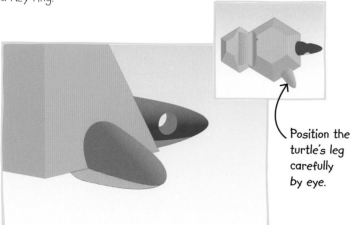

Position the turtle's leg carefully by eye.

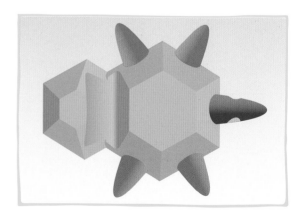

15 Rotate the paraboloid so its circular end faces one of the sides of the turtle's body. Slide it into the body so it overlaps by about 0.177 in (4.5 mm).

16 Make three copies of the leg and repeat **step 15** to put them all in position.

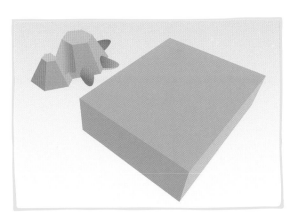

17 Make a box large enough to cover your entire model. Place it next to the turtle to make sure the box is bigger than the turtle.

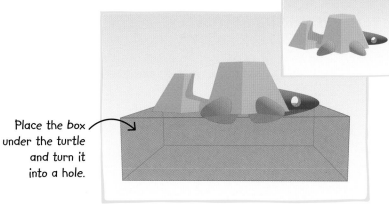

Place the box under the turtle and turn it into a hole.

18 Move the box below the work plane and under the model. Turn it into a hole to trim the parts of the model that lie under the work plane. This gives your turtle a flat base.

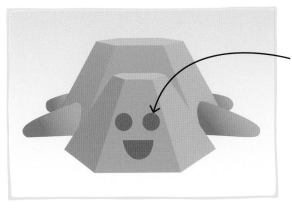

Keep the eyes and the mouth close to the body to print without supports.

19 If you like, add extra shapes to give your turtle a face. Save your model and open the file in your **slicer** program. It won't need any supports. Set the infill to 15–20 percent.

NOW TRY THIS

You can adapt this model to make different kinds of animals. Try using spheres to make a ladybird, for instance. You can even turn your turtle into a dragon by adding spikes, but don't make them too sharp!

Painted head and spots

Ladybird phone stand

Dragon phone stand and key ring

The hole for the key ring will print without any supports.

SHARK PHONE STAND

Inspired by the jaws of a great white shark, this phone stand is big enough to hold a tablet computer in its teeth. Take care to get the angle of the slot just right to make sure your stand is stable.

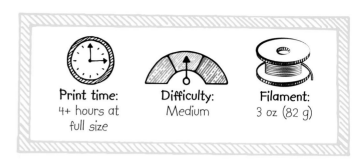

Print time:
4+ hours at full size

Difficulty:
Medium

Filament:
3 oz (82 g)

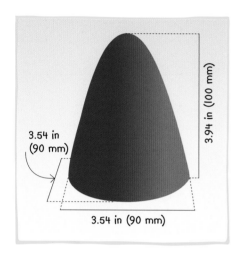

3.94 in (100 mm)

3.54 in (90 mm)

3.54 in (90 mm)

1 To create the shark's head, start by putting a paraboloid on the work plane. Resize it to match the dimensions given here.

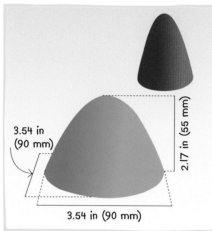

3.54 in (90 mm)

2.17 in (55 mm)

3.54 in (90 mm)

2 Add a second paraboloid and make it shorter, using the dimensions shown above.

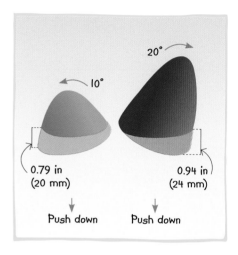

20°

10°

0.79 in (20 mm)

0.94 in (24 mm)

Push down   Push down

3 Rotate the smaller paraboloid to the left by 10 degrees and the taller one to the right by 20 degrees. Then push them below the work plane, as shown here.

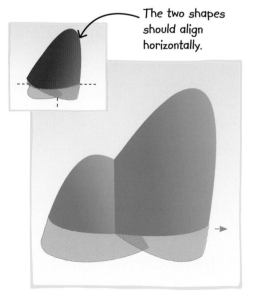

The two shapes should align horizontally.

4 Use the align tool to center the shapes horizontally but not vertically. They'll overlap each other. Hold shift and move the taller paraboloid to the right by 0.98 in (25 mm). Combine the shapes.

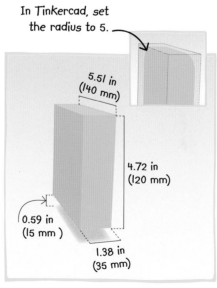

In Tinkercad, set the radius to 5.

5.51 in (140 mm)

4.72 in (120 mm)

0.59 in (15 mm)

1.38 in (35 mm)

5 To create the **slot**, take a box and resize it to match the dimensions here. Make the edges rounded if your 3D program lets you, and raise it 0.59 in (15 mm) above the work plane.

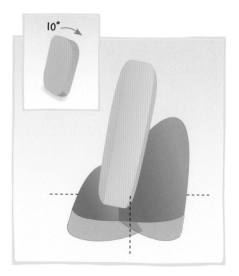

10°

6 Rotate the box to the right by 10 degrees. Then use the align tool to center it with the shark without moving it vertically.

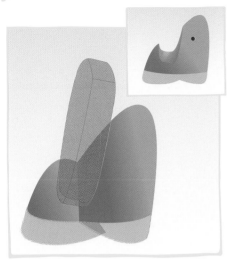

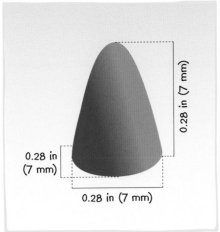

7 Next, turn the box into a hole. You can now see the jaws of the shark as well as your phone slot. Add small spheres for the **eyes**.

8 To make a **tooth** for your shark, select a paraboloid and resize it to 0.28 in (7 mm) tall, wide, and deep.

9 Place the paraboloid inside a jaw and push it in slightly. Make copies and space these evenly inside the shark's mouth.

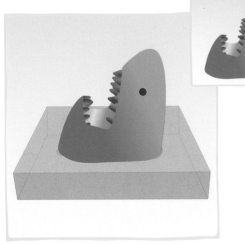

11 Import the file into your **slicer** program. As there are no large overhangs, you may not need supports. After the model has printed, you could paint the eyes and teeth to make them stand out.

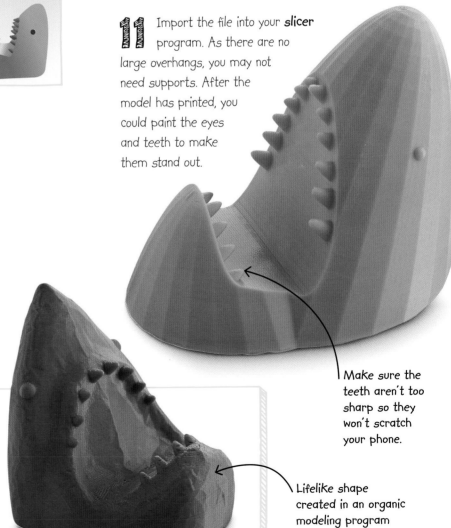

10 Select another box and move it under the shark's head, placing it below the work plane. Make it wider than the shark and then turn it into a hole. This gives your shark a flat base.

Make sure the teeth aren't too sharp so they won't scratch your phone.

Lifelike shape created in an organic modeling program

NOW TRY THIS

You can build a more lifelike shark with an organic modeling program. To give it a perfectly flat base, import your organic model into a geometric modeling program and remove the bottom layer.

Evenly spaced holes
make the best pattern.

STAR
LANTERN

Light up your room with this
dazzling lantern, which glows in
the dark and casts starry lights
on the walls. The stars are made
by using a repeating shape to cut
holes out of a sphere. You can use
any shape you like if you want to
customize the lantern and make
different patterns of light.

HOW TO CREATE A
STAR LANTERN

You'll need a bright, battery-operated LED for this easy project. It also helps to use a pale-colored filament so that light filters through the globe and makes it glow. If you don't have an LED light, make a slot in the base of the globe so you can place it over a smartphone flashlight.

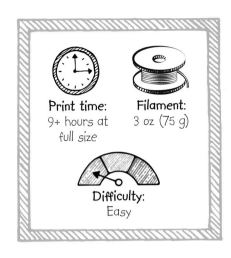

Print time:
9+ hours at full size

Filament:
3 oz (75 g)

Difficulty:
Easy

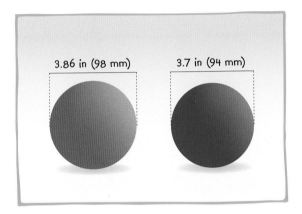

3.86 in (98 mm)   3.7 in (94 mm)

1 Place two spheres on the work plane. Hold shift and change them to the sizes shown above.

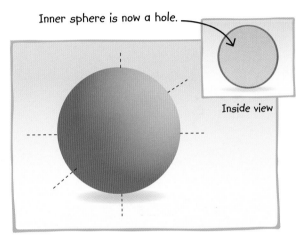

Inner sphere is now a hole.

Inside view

2 Select both spheres and use the align tool to make their centers come together. Then deselect the outer sphere and turn the inner one into a hole. You now have a hollow **globe**.

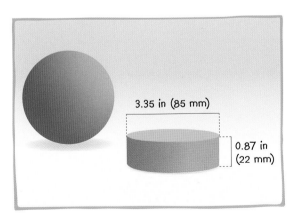

3.35 in (85 mm)

0.87 in (22 mm)

3 Add a cylinder and resize it to the dimensions above.

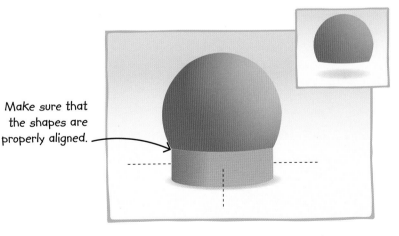

Make sure that the shapes are properly aligned.

4 Select the globe and cylinder and align their centers. Turn the cylinder into a hole so that the bottom part of the sphere disappears.

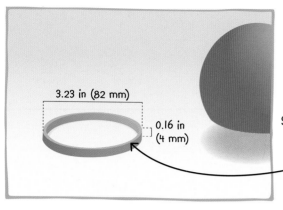

3.23 in (82 mm)

0.16 in (4 mm)

The thickness of the tube should match that of the globe.

5 Make a tube 3.23 in (82 mm) wide and 0.16 in (4 mm) tall. Then change its thickness to about 0.08 in (2 mm). In Tinkercad, you can change the shape's properties to make its "wall thickness" 0.5.

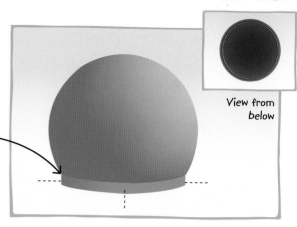

Make sure that there's no space left between the globe and the tube.

View from below

6 Select both shapes and align their centers horizontally. Move the globe down 0.71 in (18 mm) so it touches the tube. Join them to make one shape.

7 Choose a star shape from the menu. If your 3D program doesn't have a star shape, you can draw one in an illustration program and import it, or you could create one using triangles in your 3D program.

The star should be about 0.79 in (20 mm) thick.

90°

0.59 in (15 mm)

8 Make the star about 0.59 in (15 mm) tall and 0.79 in (20 mm) thick. Rotate it by a quarter turn (90 degrees) to make it stand upright.

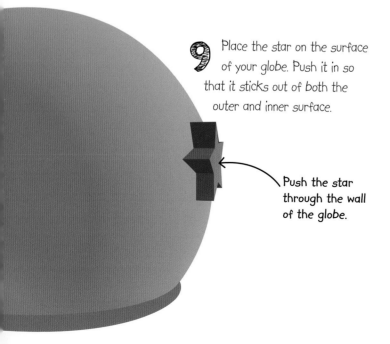

9 Place the star on the surface of your globe. Push it in so that it sticks out of both the outer and inner surface.

Push the star through the wall of the globe.

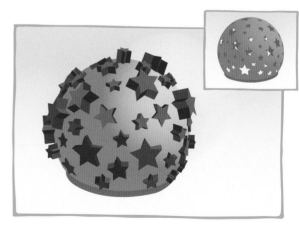

10 Make copies of the star and place them all over the globe. You'll need to rotate each one, as shown here. Then turn the stars into holes so the globe is covered in star-shaped holes.

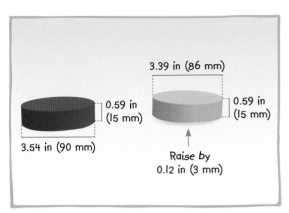

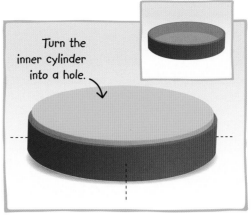

12 Select both cylinders and align their centers using only the horizontal axes. Make the inner cylinder into a hole. You now have the *base* of your star lantern.

11 To make a **base** for your globe, take two cylinders of different sizes, matching the dimensions given here. Raise the smaller cylinder 0.12 in (3 mm) *above the work plane.*

WARNING: Do not use real flames inside this globe.

13 Save the globe and *base* as two separate files. Open the *globe* in your **slicer** program. You'll need supports and a raft to print the *globe* properly.

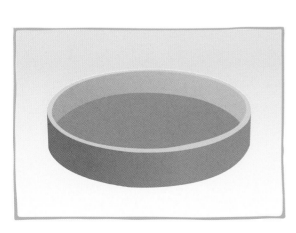

LED light

14 Open the base file in the slicer program. As there are no overhangs, the base won't need supports. The *globe* needs supports, and should be printed separately.

15 Your lantern will work *best* with a powerful LED light. Don't use a candle as the flame will *set fire* to the plastic. Try the lantern in a dark room with plain walls to see it at its best!

PLANT POT

These plant pots are the perfect gift for someone with green fingers. They are designed for miniature plants like herbs and cacti and have holes in the top for string. To add interest, you can put decorative features on the surface—anything from a name to a pair of legs!

Use string to hang your plant pot.

Cacti work well in these small pots as they don't need watering often.

Leave out surface decorations if you want a simple, smooth plant pot.

Paint the ribs a different color.

Create legs using basic geometric shapes.

HOW TO CREATE A
PLANT POT

The main part of the plant pot is a hollow oval and is easy to make. Be careful to get the three holes for string in the right places so the pot isn't crooked when it hangs. If you want to adapt the plant pot to stand instead of hang, you'll need to change the rounded base to a flat one. You could also add a drainage hole for water.

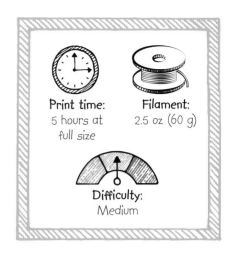

Print time:
5 hours at
full size

Filament:
2.5 oz (60 g)

Difficulty:
Medium

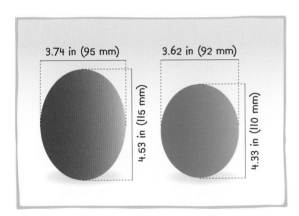

3.74 in (95 mm)   3.62 in (92 mm)

4.53 in (115 mm)   4.33 in (110 mm)

1 Place two spheres on the work plane. Holding shift, change their diameters to 3.74 in (95 mm) and 3.62 in (92 mm). Then, without holding shift, increase their heights to 4.53 in (115 mm) and 4.33 in (110 mm), respectively.

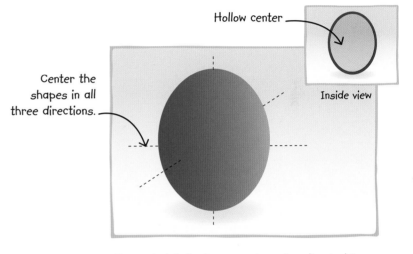

Hollow center

Center the shapes in all three directions.

Inside view

2 Select both shapes and use the align tool to center them along the lines shown. Deselect the outer sphere, turn the inner one into a hole, and combine.

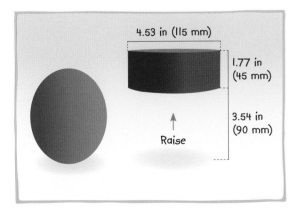

4.53 in (115 mm)

1.77 in (45 mm)

3.54 in (90 mm)

Raise

3 Take a cylinder and resize it, holding shift, until its diameter is 4.53 in (115 mm). Then make it 1.77 in (45 mm) tall and place it 3.54 in (90 mm) above the work plane.

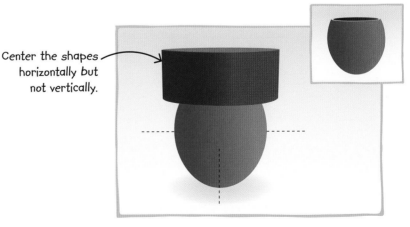

Center the shapes horizontally but not vertically.

4 Center the two objects as shown here. Then turn the cylinder into a hole to make an opening at the top. The main part of the plant pot is now complete.

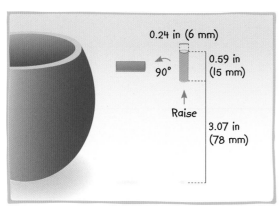

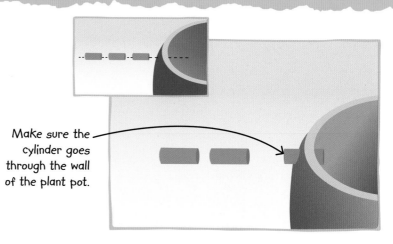

Make sure the cylinder goes through the wall of the plant pot.

5 Take a cylinder and make it 0.24 in (6 mm) wide and 0.59 in (15 mm) tall. Raise it 3.07 in (78 mm) above the work plane and then rotate it by 90 degrees.

6 Make two copies of the cylinder and then use the align tool to center them all with the pot. While holding shift, slide the first cylinder through the wall of the pot so that it sticks out on both sides.

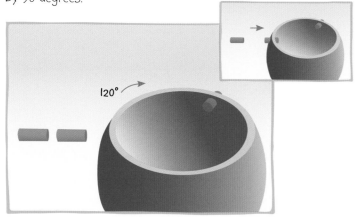

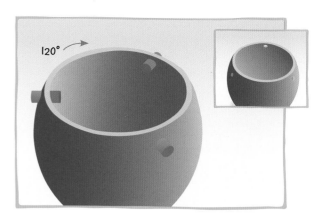

7 Select the plant pot and the first cylinder, and rotate both clockwise by 120 degrees. Hold shift and slide the second cylinder through the wall of the pot so that it sticks out on both sides.

8 Repeat **step 7** to insert the third cylinder into the pot as shown. Then turn all the cylinders into holes.

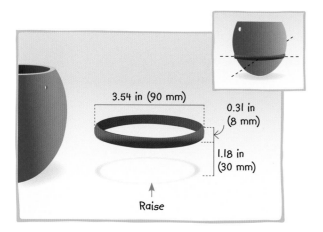

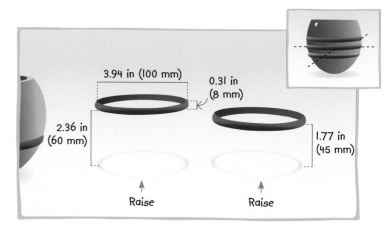

9 You can now decorate your plant pot. To add a rib, make a ring as shown. Raise it 1.18 in (30 mm) above the work plane and then use the align tool to center it with the plant pot.

10 Take another ring, but this time match the dimensions given above. Make a copy of it. Raise both above the work plane, with one sitting at a height of 2.36 in (60 mm) and the other at 1.77 in (45 mm). Center the rings with the pot.

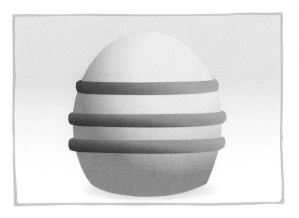

11 Save your file and then open it in a **slicer** program. This plant pot can be printed without supports if you print it upside down. Set the infill to about 10 percent.

NOW TRY THIS

The basic shape of the plant pot can be adapted to build other interesting models. To create legs for your plant pot, first stretch a semicircle to make a thigh. Then use another semicircle and a half sphere to make a foot. Give the plant pot a flat base so it will stand up.

Half sphere

Semicircle

Flat base

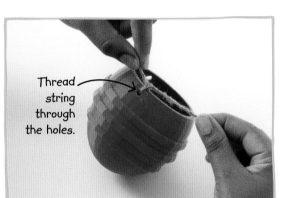

Thread string through the holes.

12 When the pot is printed, take three pieces of string and pass them through the holes at the top. Tie them in a knot at the top to hang your pot from a hook or other support.

Tie the three pieces of string together.

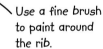

Use a fine brush to paint around the rib.

13 If you added decorations to your plant pot, painting them a different color will make them stand out.

Acrylic craft paint

FRIDGE MAGNET

This froggy fridge magnet takes under an hour to print and is very handy for sticking pictures, postcards, and notes to a fridge door. To create the frog's natural shape, you'll need an organic modeling program such as Sculptris. This allows you to mold a 3D object in the same way a sculptor works with clay. Follow the steps as closely as you can, but don't worry if your frog turns out different—it won't look exactly like the one in the book!

Football match at 5!

Make Fridge magnet ✓
Build castle
Fix racing car
Camping

HOW TO CREATE A
FRIDGE MAGNET

There are two different stages in this project. The first stage shows you how to sculpt a frog using an organic modeling program. The second shows you how to import your sculpture into a geometric modeling program to give it a perfectly flat base. You'll need a stick-on magnet if you want to make your frog sticky.

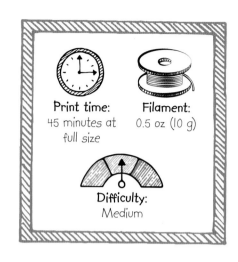

Print time:
45 minutes at full size

Filament:
0.5 oz (10 g)

Difficulty:
Medium

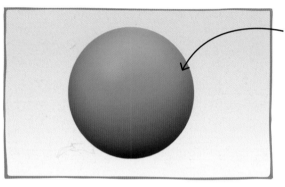

Organic modeling projects typically start with a ball of virtual "clay."

1 Start a new project in an organic modeling program such as Sculptris. Make sure symmetry is turned on. This ensures that changes to one side of the model are mirrored on the other.

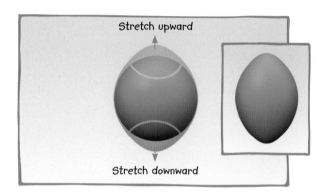

Stretch upward

Stretch downward

2 Select the grab tool and adjust its size to match the yellow guide shown here. Select the top of the sphere and pull it upward. Repeat at the bottom. Make sure you pick points right in the middle. Try to match the small picture. If you find it difficult, click undo and try again.

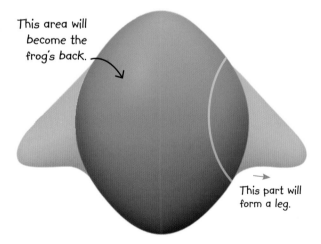

This area will become the frog's back.

This part will form a leg.

3 Next we'll make the **front legs**. Grab a point on the side and stretch it outward and downward. A leg will form on both sides.

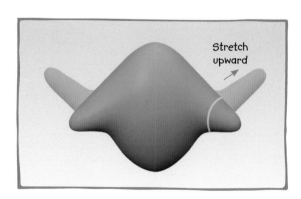

Stretch upward

4 Reduce the size setting of the grab tool and pull the tip of a leg upward. If the legs becomes flat or pointed when they stretch, use the inflate tool to make them rounder.

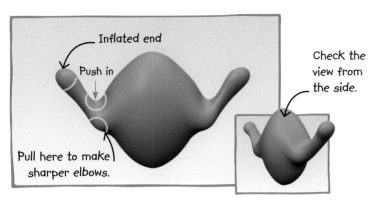

Inflated end

Push in

Pull here to make sharper elbows.

Check the view from the side.

5 To make the legs more realistic, use the grab tool to make a crease at the base and to pull out the elbow a little. Then use the inflate tool to make the ends of the legs rounder.

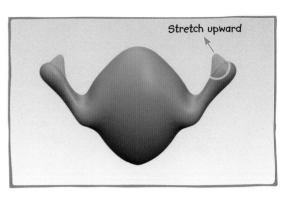

Stretch upward

6 To make a toe, grab the inflated end of a leg and pull it upward, as shown above.

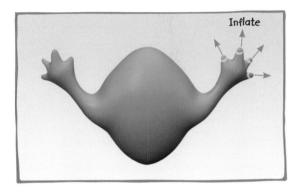

Inflate

7 Repeat **step 6** until there are four toes on each leg. Inflate the tips of the toes to make them rounder.

The shape should look like this from the side.

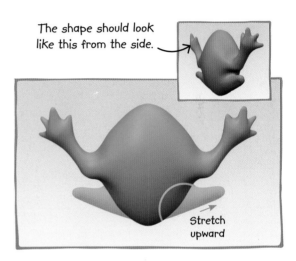

Stretch upward

8 Grab the lower part of the body and pull it to the right and slightly upward.

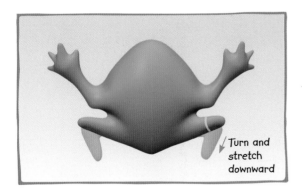

Turn and stretch downward

9 To make knees, select the end of the leg and pull it down with the grab tool. You can adjust the shape of the **hind legs** further by using the grab tool.

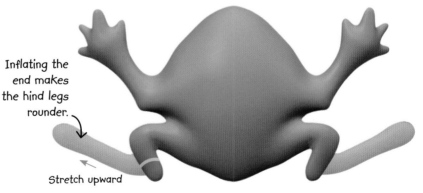

Inflating the end makes the hind legs rounder.

Stretch upward

10 To make feet, grab and stretch the end of one leg. Use the inflate tool to make it rounder if it becomes pointed or oddly shaped.

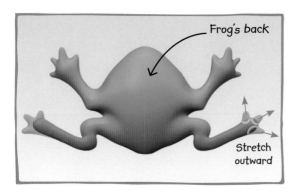

11 Repeat **steps** 6 and 7 to make the toes for the hind legs. Each hind leg should have three toes. As before, use the inflate tool to make the toe tips rounder.

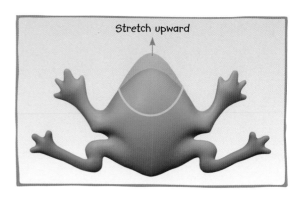

12 To create the **head**, grab a large area at the top of the body and pull it upward.

13 To add the eyes, grab and then inflate a small area on one side of the head.

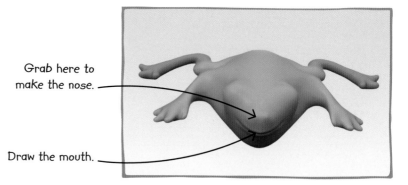

14 Flip the frog over so he's facing you, with his belly underneath. Starting in the middle, use the crease tool to draw a mouth. Then use the grab tool to make bumps for nostrils.

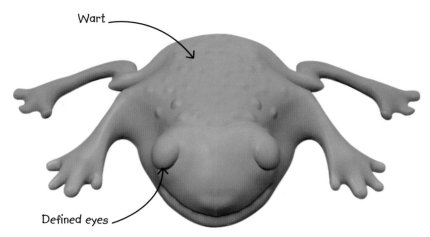

15 Finally, use the crease tool to enhance the eyes, and then the grab tool to add small warts on the back. Export the model as an .obj or .stl file to use in a geometric modeling program.

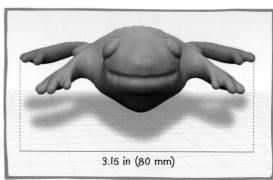

16 When you open the file in your geometric modeling program, the frog may be too big or small. Hold shift and resize it to about 3.15 in (80 mm) wide.

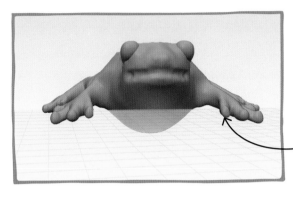

17 Push the frog down to move the rounded part of the belly under the work plane. If the feet are too low, go back to Sculptris and adjust them.

The feet should only touch the work plane. Make sure they don't sink in further.

18 Enlarge a box so it's bigger than the frog and move it under the frog and under the work plane. Turn it into a hole to make the base of the frog completely flat. If you don't have a self-adhesive magnet, make a hole in the frog's base for a solid magnet.

19 The model can be printed without supports and with 15 percent infill. To complete your magnet, stick a self-adhesive magnet to the frog's base. If you're using a solid magnet, ask an adult to glue it into the hole.

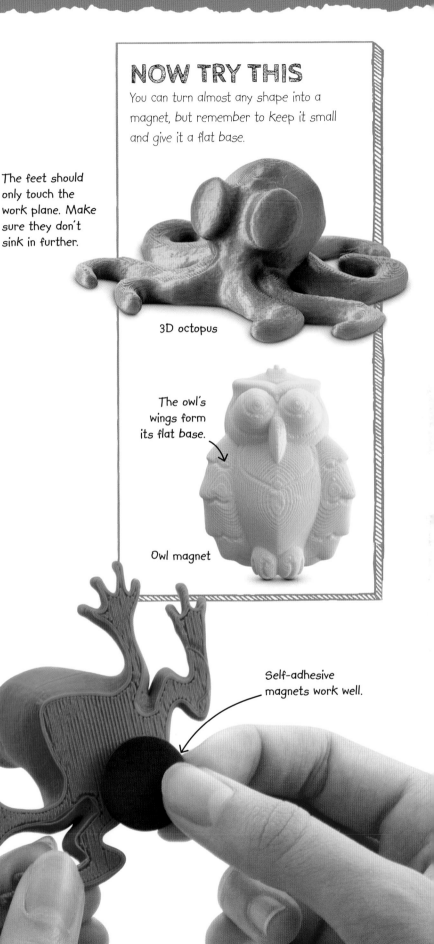

NOW TRY THIS

You can turn almost any shape into a magnet, but remember to keep it small and give it a flat base.

3D octopus

The owl's wings form its flat base.

Owl magnet

Self-adhesive magnets work well.

RACE CAR

With a bit of care and ingenuity, you can design and print 3D models that have moving parts, such as wheels, joints, and gears. These race cars have wheels that turn freely on their axles, allowing you to race them for real. You can use the same mechanism to create any kind of toy vehicle, from a monster truck to a train.

Print wheels in black to make them realistic.

Axle

Wheel

HOW TO CREATE A
RACE CAR

This model car is made of lots of separate parts that are assembled after being printed. Make sure you use the correct dimensions for the wheels, axles, and washers. The washers are designed to fit tightly on the axles, while the wheels and axles are loose to allow them to turn.

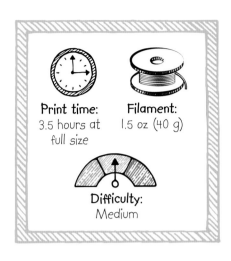

Print time:
3.5 hours at full size

Filament:
1.5 oz (40 g)

Difficulty:
Medium

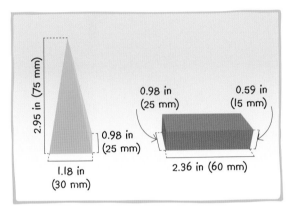

1 To make the **body** of the race car, start with a pyramid and a box. Resize them to match the dimensions in the picture.

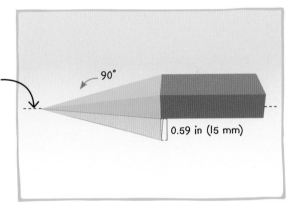

Center the objects along the dotted line shown here.

90°

0.59 in (15 mm)

2 Rotate the pyramid as shown and push it down so that 0.59 in (15 mm) of the model sits below the work plane. Then join the flat side of the pyramid with the shorter side of the box, and align the shapes as shown above.

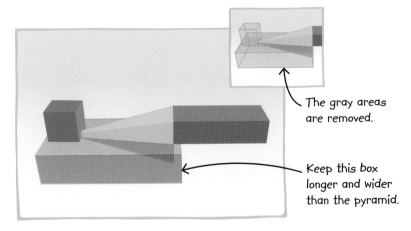

The gray areas are removed.

Keep this box longer and wider than the pyramid.

3 Use a small box to cover the front 0.79 in (20 mm) of the pyramid. Then place a larger box under the model to cover the part of the pyramid below the work plane. Turn these two boxes into holes, and then combine all the shapes.

0.47 in (12 mm)

0.20 in (5 mm)

0.39 in (10 mm)

0.51 in (13 mm)

Raise

4 Now take a wedge. Turn it upside down and resize it to match the shape shown here. Raise the wedge to place it 0.51 in (13 mm) above the work plane.

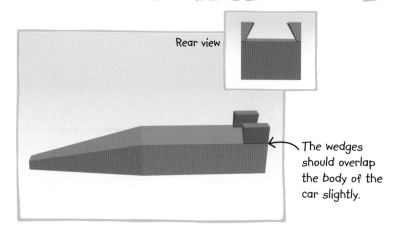

Rear view

The wedges should overlap the body of the car slightly.

5 Make a copy of the wedge and either rotate it or flip it to make a mirror image. Place both wedges at the rear corners of the car.

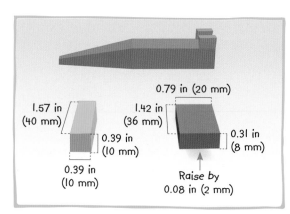

0.79 in (20 mm)

1.57 in (40 mm)

1.42 in (36 mm)

0.39 in (10 mm)

0.31 in (8 mm)

0.39 in (10 mm)

Raise by 0.08 in (2 mm)

6 Next we'll create **wings**. Use two boxes of different sizes (see above). Raise the wider box 0.08 in (2 mm) above the work plane.

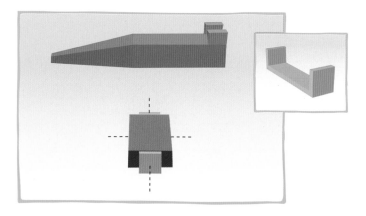

7 Align the centers of the two boxes along the lines shown above. Take care not to move the boxes vertically. Turn the wider box into a hole. The front wing is now ready.

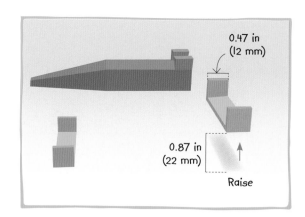

0.47 in (12 mm)

0.87 in (22 mm)

Raise

8 For the rear wing, make a copy of the front wing and enlarge it slightly while holding shift to make it 0.47 in (12 mm) wide. Raise it 0.87 in (22 mm) above the work plane.

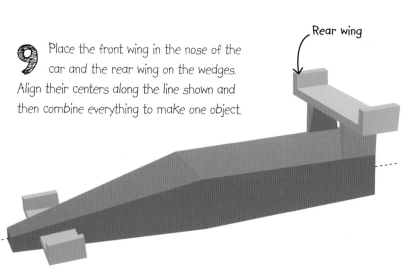

Rear wing

9 Place the front wing in the nose of the car and the rear wing on the wedges. Align their centers along the line shown and then combine everything to make one object.

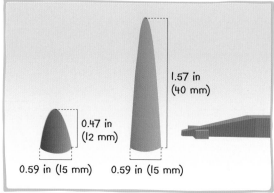

1.57 in (40 mm)

0.47 in (12 mm)

0.59 in (15 mm)   0.59 in (15 mm)

10 Next take two paraboloids and resize them to match the dimensions shown above. These will make **air intakes**.

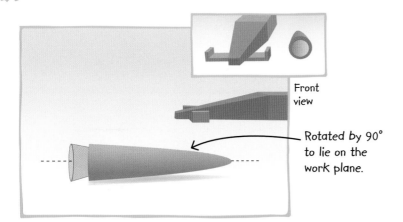

Front view

Rotated by 90° to lie on the work plane.

11 Rotate the two paraboloids by 90 degrees. Place about half of the shorter paraboloid inside the other and align them as shown. Turn the shorter paraboloid into a hole.

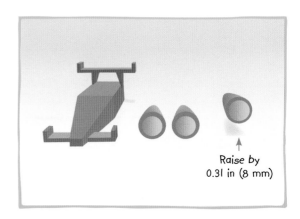

Raise by 0.31 in (8 mm)

12 Make two copies of the air intake. Raise one of them so it sits 0.31 in (8 mm) above the work plane.

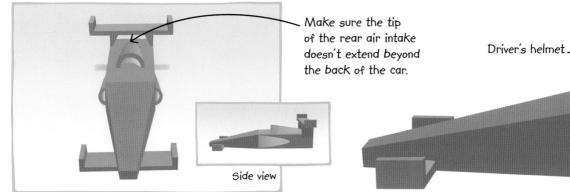

Make sure the tip of the rear air intake doesn't extend beyond the back of the car.

Side view

13 Move the raised air intake horizontally to place it near the rear end of the car. Embed the other two on either side of the car, so that less than half of each paraboloid sticks out. Combine the shapes to create the car's body.

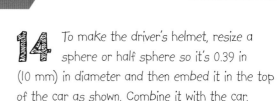

Driver's helmet

14 To make the driver's helmet, resize a sphere or half sphere so it's 0.39 in (10 mm) in diameter and then embed it in the top of the car as shown. Combine it with the car.

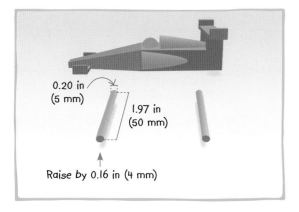

0.20 in (5 mm)

1.97 in (50 mm)

Raise by 0.16 in (4 mm)

15 Next you need to make holes for the wheel axles. Take a cylinder and rotate it to lie on the work plane. Resize it as shown. Then raise it 0.16 in (4 mm) above the work plane and make a copy.

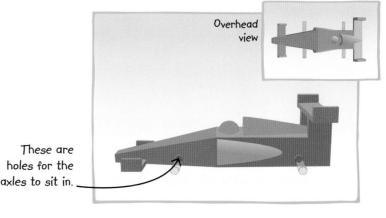

Overhead view

These are holes for the axles to sit in.

16 Embed the cylinders in the car, one in the front part and the other near the rear. Make sure each cylinder sticks out on either side. Turn the cylinders into holes.

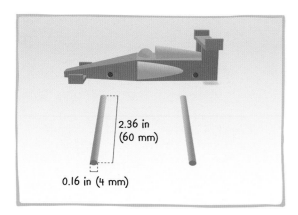

17 To make the **axles**, create a cylinder with the dimensions shown here, and then make a copy of it. These are 0.04 in (1 mm) narrower than the holes to allow them to move freely.

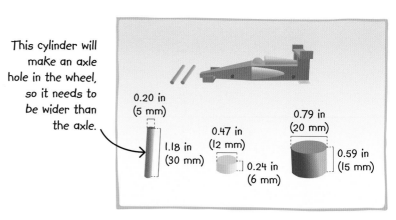

18 Create cylinders of different sizes (purple, yellow, and blue, above) to make a **wheel** for the car.

This cylinder will make an axle hole in the wheel, so it needs to be wider than the axle.

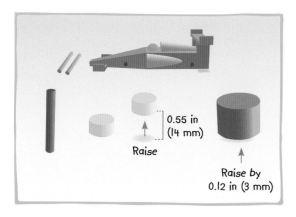

19 Raise the blue cylinder so it sits 0.12 in (3 mm) above the work plane. Make a copy of the yellow cylinder and lift it 0.55 in (14 mm) above the work plane.

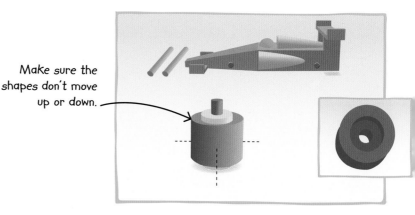

Make sure the shapes don't move up or down.

20 Align all the centers of the shapes without moving them vertically. Then select the purple and yellow cylinders and turn them into holes. You've built a wheel.

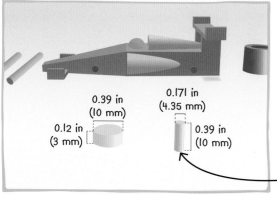

21 You'll need **washers** to keep your wheels and axles in place. So take two cylinders and resize them as shown above.

This cylinder makes a hole in the washer. If your printed washer is too loose or tight, adjust this cylinder's diameter.

22 Center the cylinders horizontally and vertically. Turn the inner cylinder into a hole. Your washer is now ready.

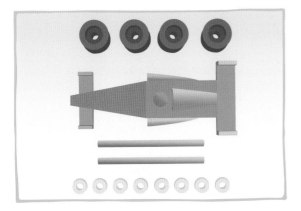

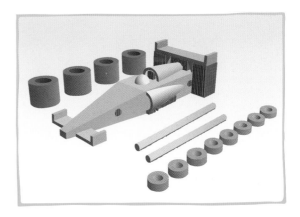

23 Copy the wheel and the washer so you have four wheels and eight washers in total. Arrange all the parts so they sit exactly on the work plane without touching each other. Your race car is now ready to print! Save as an .obj or .stl file.

24 Open the file in your **slicer** program and set the infill to 15 percent. You can print all the parts together. Add supports to the rear wing, air intakes, axles, axle holes, and wheels. If your slicer software can create treelike supports, use these rather than linear supports.

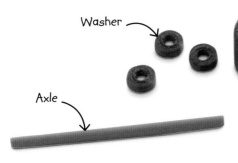

25 Carefully remove the supports, especially under the wings and from the axles and their holes.

Washer

Axle

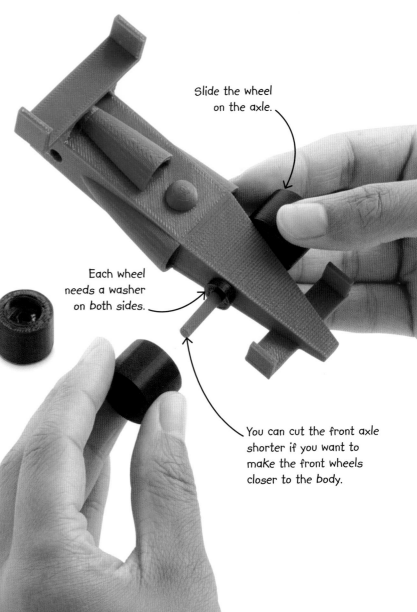

Slide the wheel on the axle.

Each wheel needs a washer on both sides.

You can cut the front axle shorter if you want to make the front wheels closer to the body.

26 Slide the axles into their holes and add the washers and wheels. If the washers don't grip the axles tightly, ask an adult to glue them to the axles or use some sticky tack to hold them in place. Take care not to stick the wheels to the axles or the axles to the car.

TROLL FAMILY

Creating monsters with an organic modeling program is a great way to let your imagination go wild. You can make the body any shape and add as many eyes as you like! This project shows you how to make a troll that you can adapt to create a whole family, but you can use the same techniques for any mythical being.

Baby troll

Ugg!!

HOW TO CREATE A
TROLL FAMILY

You'll need an organic modeling program for the main part of this project and a geometric modeling program for the last few steps, where you make the base of the feet flat. If you aren't used to organic modeling, try to follow the steps closely—doing this will teach you how the different tools work. As you build your model, turn it around occasionally so you can check how it looks from different angles.

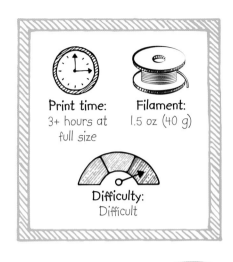

Print time:
3+ hours at full size

Filament:
1.5 oz (40 g)

Difficulty:
Difficult

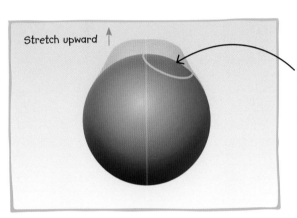

Stretch upward

Select the grab tool and adjust its size to match this yellow guide.

1 To start making a **face**, use the grab tool to pull an area near the top of the sphere upward. Make sure symmetry is turned on so your changes affect both sides at once.

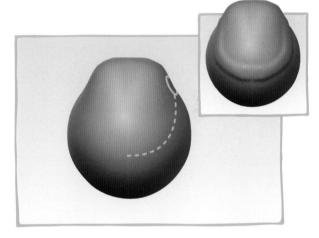

2 Switch to the draw tool. Adjust the brush size to match the yellow circle above and then use the draw tool to create a raised area along the dotted line. This will form the outline of the face.

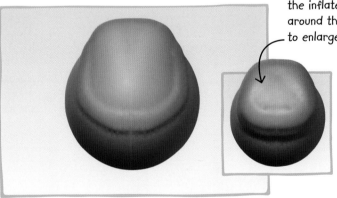

Holding your mouse button down, drag the inflate tool around the face to enlarge it.

3 Now use the inflate tool to enlarge the whole area of the face. Keep using it until you have a bulky, rounded shape, as shown in the small picture.

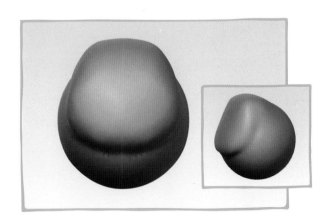

4 If the face looks lumpy or uneven, use the smooth tool to even it out. You can rotate your model in a different direction to check you're happy with the shape.

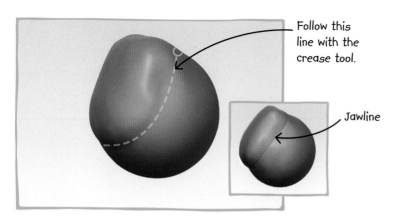

Follow this line with the crease tool.

Jawline

5 To give the head a more well-defined jawline, turn it sideways and use the crease tool to draw around the jaw and chin. Then smooth out any flaws.

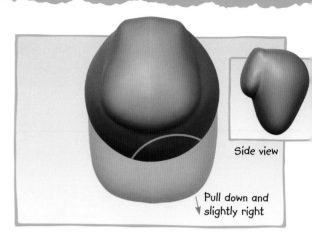

Side view

Pull down and slightly right

6 We'll make the **torso** next. Turn the model back around to face you. Select the grab tool and set its size to match the yellow circle. Pull the marked area down and slightly to the right.

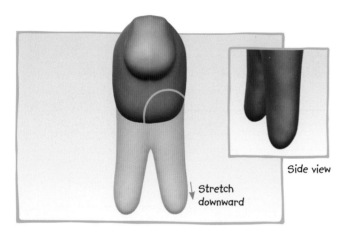

Side view

Stretch downward

7 Now use the grab tool to create the **legs**. If they're too thin, use the inflate tool to make them fatter. Then use the smooth tool to smooth out any uneven parts.

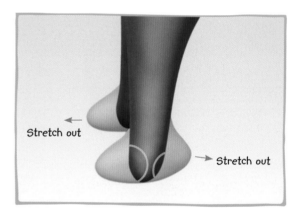

Stretch out

Stretch out

8 Rotate the model to face left. To create feet, use the grab tool to extend the bottom of each leg forward and backward. Then inflate the ends and smooth any uneven edges.

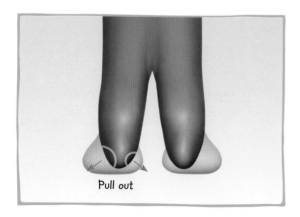

Pull out

9 Rotate the model to the front to finish shaping the feet. Use the grab tool to pull the areas in the guides.

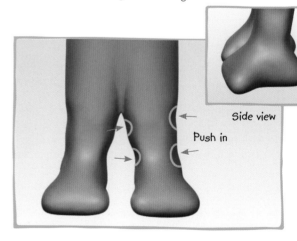

Side view

Push in

10 Continue using the grab tool to refine the shape of the legs and feet by pushing in at the points shown.

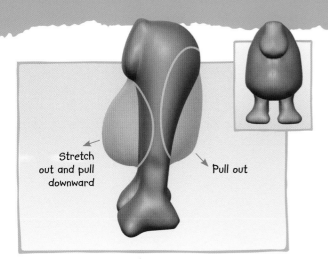

11 Turn the model sideways again. Use the grab tool to create a bulging belly. Then increase the grab tool's size to match the yellow guide at the back, and pull outward to make a rounded back.

12 Turn the model to face you and use the grab tool to create **arms**. Increase the strength of the tool if it doesn't pull out enough material. Use the inflate tool to fatten the arms if needed and the smooth tool to refine their shape.

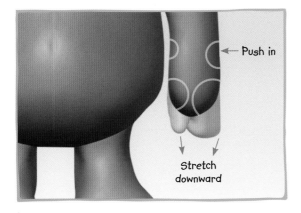

13 Using the grab tool, push inward at the top yellow circles and pull down at the bottom circles. This defines the wrist. Then use inflate to enlarge the fist and grab to lengthen the thumb.

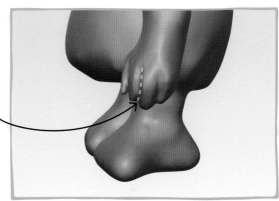

14 Turn the model sideways. Using the crease tool, make creases between the fingers. You can also use the grab tool to push in parts of the fist.

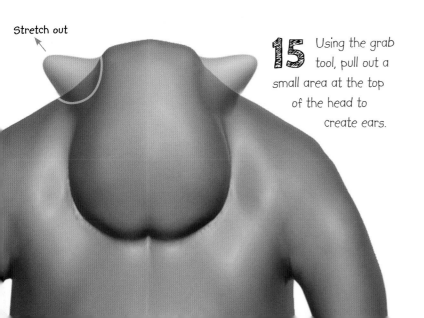

15 Using the grab tool, pull out a small area at the top of the head to create ears.

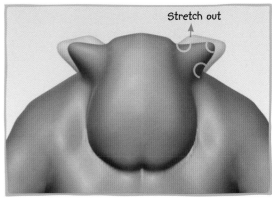

16 If the ears look too thin or pointy, inflate them. To improve their shape further, grab and stretch the areas highlighted here.

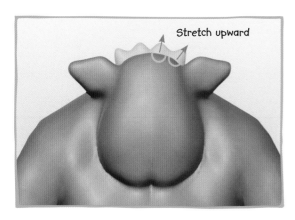

Stretch upward

17 To add hair, reduce the size of the grab tool and pull up small areas at the top of the head. Don't make the hair too fine or it won't print properly.

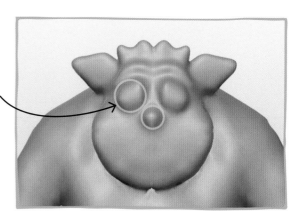

Use inflate to make the eyes and nose.

18 Adjust the inflate tool to match the yellow guides in the picture. Then use it to shape the troll's eyes and nose.

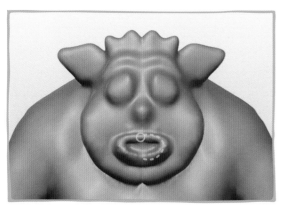

19 Use the draw tool to create lips around the mouth.

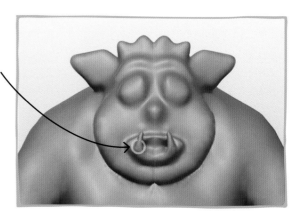

Avoid thin, sharp tusks, as they may not print properly.

20 Using the grab tool, pull out a small part of the mouth to create tusks, but don't make the tips sharp. Save your model.

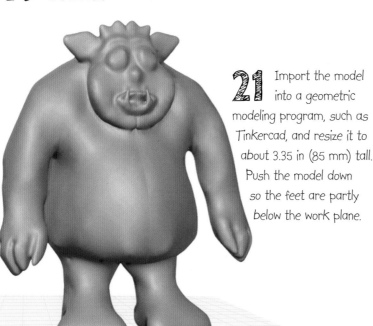

21 Import the model into a geometric modeling program, such as Tinkercad, and resize it to about 3.35 in (85 mm) tall. Push the model down so the feet are partly below the work plane.

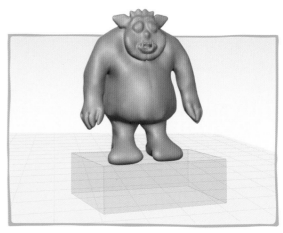

22 Place a box directly under the work plane and, if necessary, make it wider so it covers the area the troll is standing on.

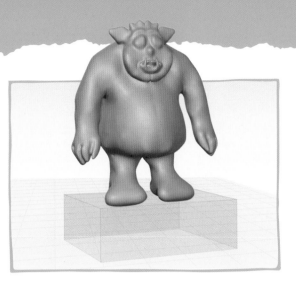

Back view

Supports

Brim

23 Turn the box into a hole. This trims the part of the model below the work plane, giving the troll a flat surface. Save the file.

24 Open the file in your **slicer** program. Add supports for the arms and a brim or raft to support the model. Set the infill to 15 percent.

25 Once the model has printed, you'll need to carefully remove the supports. Be especially gentle with the arms as they might break when you pull the supports off. If the supports are tricky to remove, ask an adult to help.

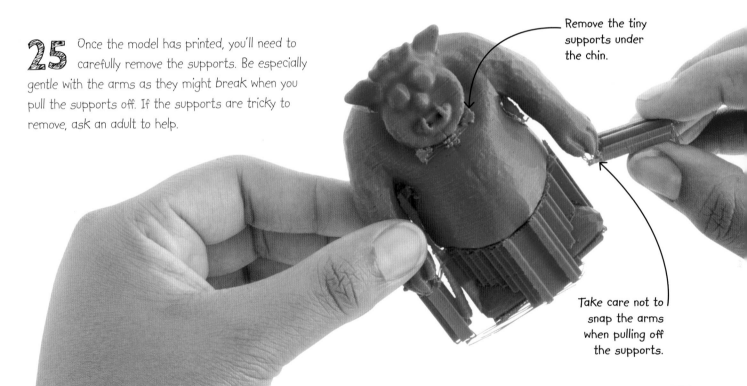

Remove the tiny supports under the chin.

Take care not to snap the arms when pulling off the supports.

3D MINI-ME

A skilled digital sculptor can make realistic human figures, but a much quicker way to model the human body accurately is to use a 3D scanner. This creates a stunning, lifelike model called a "mini-me"— like a 3D photograph.

Photos taken from lots of directions are combined to make a 3D model.

The model is printed in full color using sandstone.

CHESS SET

3D printers are great for making small figures such as chess pieces. This project shows you how to make a standard chess set from simple shapes in a geometric modeling program. Once you've mastered how to make this set, why not make your own personalized version. You could even use an organic modeling program to create a chess set made of monsters or wizards.

You can create your own chess board with a piece of paper or cardboard.

HOW TO CREATE A
CHESS SET

To make this chess set easier to build, all the models have the same base, which you only have to build once. The tops are then adapted to make pawns, rooks, knights, and bishops, as well as a queen and king. You'll need to print two sets of pieces in different colors to make a full chess set.

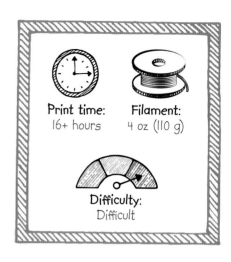

Print time: 16+ hours

Filament: 4 oz (110 g)

Difficulty: Difficult

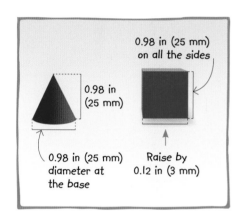

1 To make the **base** for your chess pieces, resize a cone and a cube to the dimensions shown here. Raise the cube by 0.12 in (3 mm).

0.98 in (25 mm) on all the sides

0.98 in (25 mm)

0.98 in (25 mm) diameter at the base

Raise by 0.12 in (3 mm)

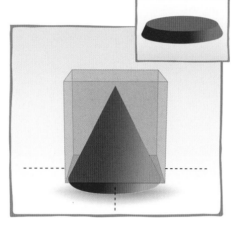

2 Select the two shapes and align their centers horizontally, as shown. Turn the box into a hole. This trims most of the cone, turning it into a disk.

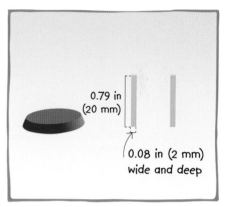

0.79 in (20 mm)

0.08 in (2 mm) wide and deep

3 Make another box 0.79 in (20 mm) tall and 0.08 in (2 mm) wide and deep. Make a copy of it.

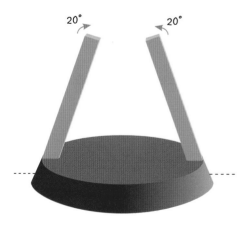

20°   20°

4 Rotate each box by 20 degrees in the directions shown. Embed the boxes at either side of the disk. Use the align tool to make sure they line up with the center of the disk.

Overhead view

5 Copy the two boxes and rotate the copied pair by 45 degrees. Keep doing this until you have eight altogether, as shown. Group them to make a single object.

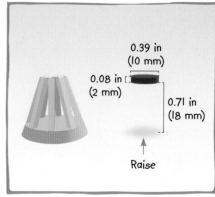

0.39 in (10 mm)

0.08 in (2 mm)

0.71 in (18 mm)

Raise

6 Make a cylinder 0.08 in (2 mm) tall and 0.39 in (10 mm) in diameter. Raise it so its base is 0.71 in (18 mm) above the work plane.

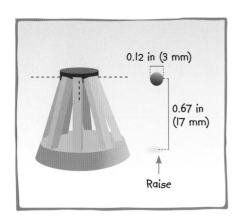

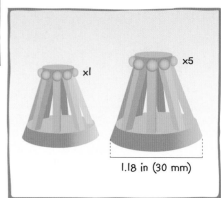

7 Place the cylinder at the top of the boxes and use the align tool to center it. Then make a sphere, as shown, and raise it above the work plane.

8 Place the sphere where a box meets the cylinder and push it in slightly. Then make copies of the sphere and place them all around.

9 Combine to make a single object, then copy and enlarge the copy as shown. Make four extra copies of the large base for later.

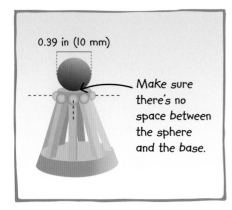

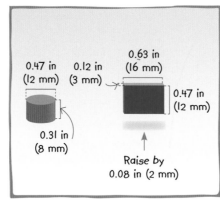

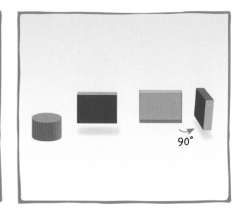

10 To create a **pawn**, make a sphere with diameter 0.39 in (10 mm) and place it on top of the shorter base from **step 9**. Align the shapes by their centers, then combine them.

11 Next, start building the head of a **rook** by resizing a cylinder and a box to the dimensions shown here. Then raise the box 0.08 in (2 mm) above the work plane.

12 Make a copy of the box and rotate it by 90 degrees. Remember to keep this new box raised over the work plane.

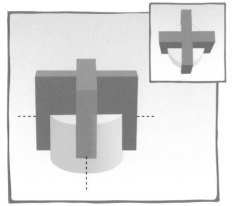

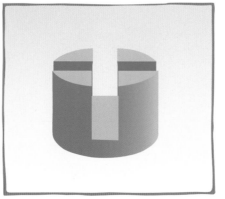

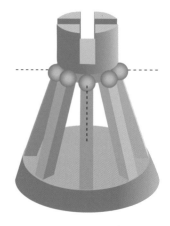

13 Select all three objects and center them horizontally. Take care not to move any shape vertically.

14 Combine the boxes into one shape and then turn it into a hole. You now have the head of a rook.

15 Place the rook's head on one of the tall bases from **step 9**. Use the align tool to center it, and then combine the shapes to form a rook.

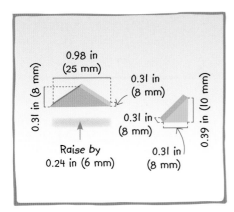

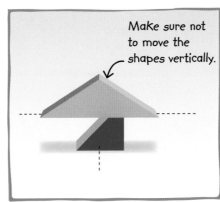

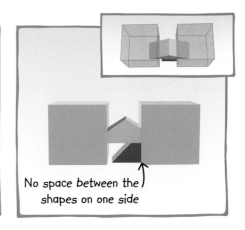

16 For the **knight's** head, resize a triangle and a wedge to the dimensions given above. Raise the triangle 0.24 in (6 mm) above the work plane.

17 Select both the shapes and use the align tool to center them as shown.

18 Place two boxes on either side of the triangle to cover the corners, matching the picture here. Turn each box into a hole.

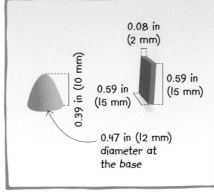

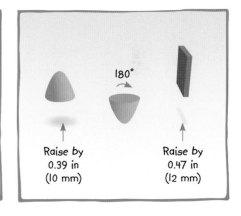

19 Combine the shapes in **step 18** to form the knight's head. Place it on top of the tall base from **step 9** and center it carefully by eye (without using the align tool).

20 To start making the head of a **bishop**, resize a paraboloid and a box to the dimensions given above. Make a copy of the paraboloid.

21 Raise one paraboloid 0.39 in (10 mm) above the work plane. Rotate the second by 180 degrees, or invert it. Next, raise the box, as shown above.

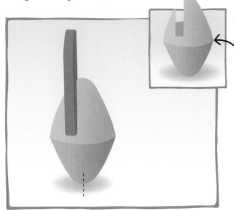

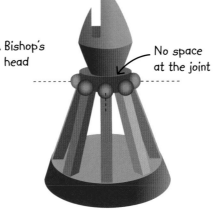

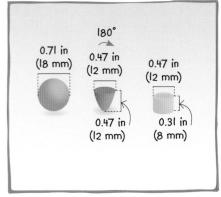

22 Align the centers of the paraboloids. Then move the box onto the top paraboloid without moving it vertically. Turn the box into a hole.

23 Position the bishop's head on top of one of the tall bases from **step 9**. Align their centers and combine the shapes. A bishop is made!

24 Next, use a sphere, an inverted paraboloid, and a tube with the dimensions given here to start making the head of a **queen**.

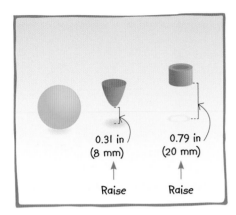

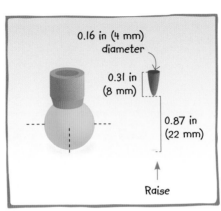

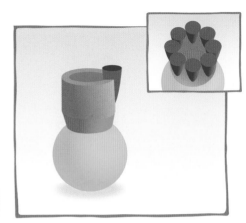

25 Raise the paraboloid and the tube to place them 0.31 in (8 mm) and 0.79 in (20 mm), respectively, above the work plane.

26 Align the centers of the shapes horizontally. Then take another paraboloid and raise it above the work plane as shown.

27 Place the paraboloid at the edge of the tube, and push it into the tube by half its width. Make copies of it and place them all around.

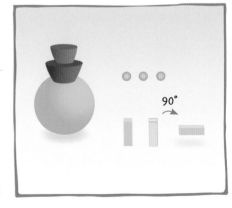

28 Combine the paraboloids into one object and then turn it into a hole. You now have a crown on the queen's head.

29 Place the queen's head on one of the tall bases from **step 9** and align their centers horizontally. Combine the shapes to end up with a queen.

30 Now for the **king's** head. Start with a sphere and two inverted paraboloids. Resize them to the dimensions given above.

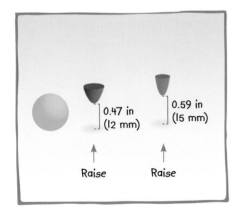

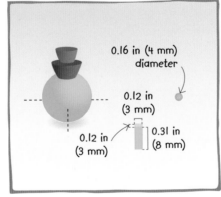

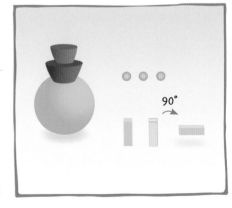

31 Raise the paraboloids so the wider one is 0.47 in (12 mm) above the work plane and the thinner one is 0.59 in (15 mm) above it.

32 Align the centers of the three shapes. Now take a box and a sphere, and resize them as shown above.

33 Make a copy of the box and rotate it by 90 degrees. Make two copies of the sphere.

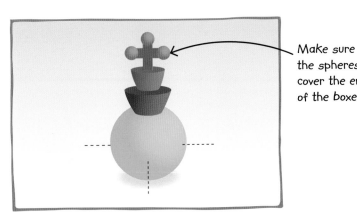

Make sure the spheres cover the ends of the boxes.

34 Place the *boxes* in a cross and put the spheres on the ends, using the align tool to make them neat. Group the spheres with the cross, then place on top of the shape from **step 32**. Center everything and combine.

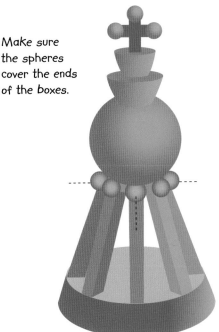

35 Place the shape from **step 34** on top of the final tall base from **step 9** and align their centers. Combine the shapes, and you have your King! Finally, make a copy of the rook, knight, and bishop so that you have two of each. Make seven extra copies of the pawn so you have eight in total. Well done, you've made a chess set!

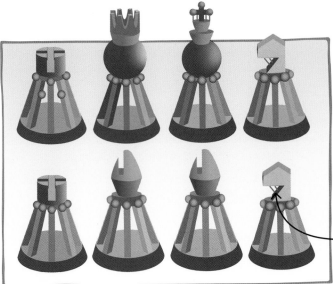

36 If the bed of your 3D printer isn't large enough to print the whole set at one time, divide them into groups. Add supports to the King and Knights in your **slicer** program. Remember, to make a full chess set you'll need to print the set twice: once in each color.

Small supports under the head of each Knight

37 If the supports are tricky to remove, ask an adult to help.

CASTLE

This medieval castle consists of over 20 parts that you can slot together in different configurations. In the center is a fortified Keep—the ideal place to imprison enemies. Surrounding it are heavily fortified ramparts and towers, with battlements to provide cover for archers. The castle even includes mini drawbridges and a portcullis to shut out invaders.

Round tower

Keep

Square tower

Battlements

Rampart

Windows

The portcullis slides
up and down.

Brick details

The drawbridges swing
open and closed.

HOW TO CREATE A
CASTLE

This large model is great fun to build but takes a long time to print. However, the ramparts and towers can slot together in different ways, allowing you to construct a smaller version of the castle if you don't have time to print everything. Gray filament works if you want the castle to look authentic or scary. Choose brighter colors if you prefer fairytale castles.

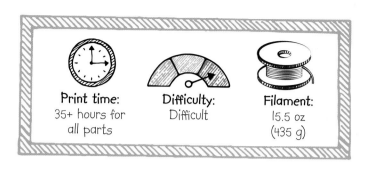

Print time: 35+ hours for all parts

Difficulty: Difficult

Filament: 15.5 oz (435 g)

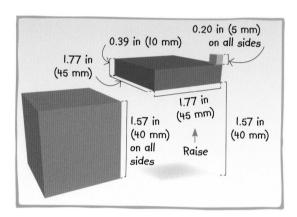

1 Start by making the **keep** (inner castle). Make three boxes matching the dimensions above. Align the smallest box on a corner of the medium one. Then raise the pair above the work plane to a height of 1.57 in (40 mm).

Place the battlements 0.20 in (5 mm) apart.

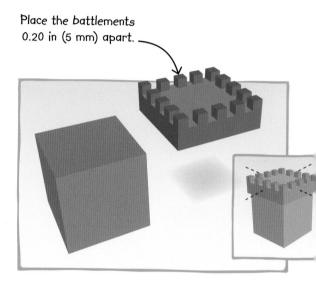

2 Make copies of the small box and, holding shift, slide the copies sideways to space them out evenly and create **battlements**. Combine them into one shape. Place it on top of the tallest box (red, above) and use the align tool to center it. Then combine everything to make a tower.

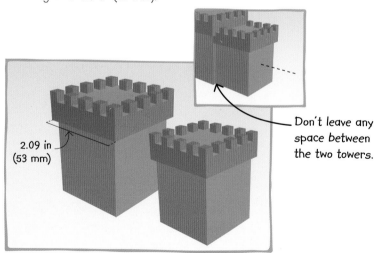

Don't leave any space between the two towers.

3 Make a copy of the tower from **step 2** and hold shift to resize it to 2.09 in (53 mm) wide. Align the two towers as shown.

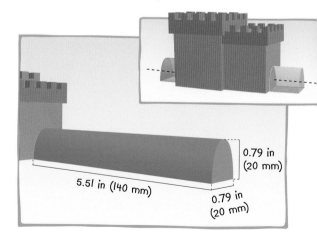

4 Take a semicircular shape and resize it as shown. Put it inside the shape from **step 3** and align their centers. Then turn the semicircular shape into a hole.

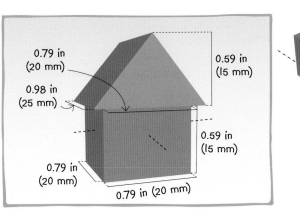

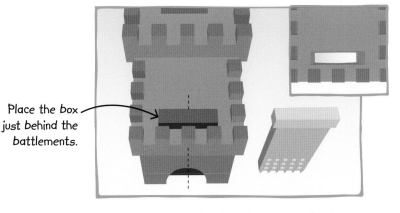

5 Take a triangle and a *box*, and then resize them using the dimensions given above. Raise the triangle 0.59 in (15 mm) to place it on the box. Align the two shapes and combine them.

6 Take the shape from **step** 5 and place it on top of the taller tower in the shape from **step 4**. Align the shapes horizontally along the line shown. Your Keep is now ready! Next we'll make a **portcullis**.

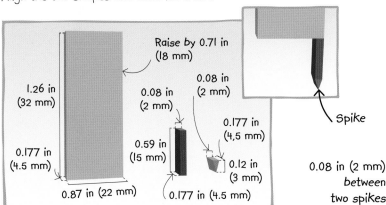

Place the big box on top of the yellow box.

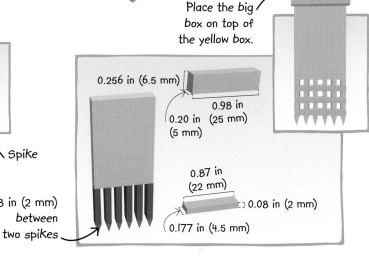

7 Take two boxes and a triangle. Flip the triangle over and then resize the shapes as shown above. Place the small box (purple) on the triangle and combine them to make a spike. Then position this under the end of the big box, which is raised.

8 Make copies of the spike and place them as above. Combine with the yellow box. Then take two boxes (gray) and resize them. Place the big one as shown. Make two copies of the small one and align all three neatly across the spikes.

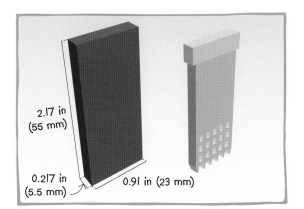

9 Combine all the shapes from **step 8**. This is your portcullis (a deadly gate that falls to the ground, impaling attacking soldiers). Take another box and resize it to match the dimensions shown here.

Place the box just behind the battlements.

10 Insert the box into the front of the keep and use the align tool to center it. Turn the box into a hole. The portcullis will fit in here.

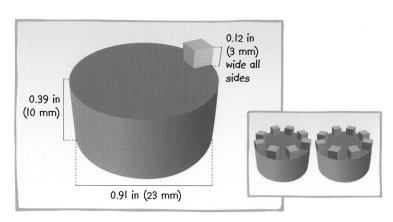

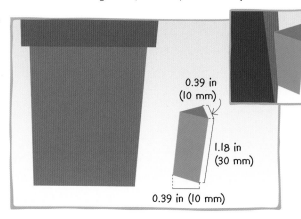

11 Take a cylinder and resize as above. Then make a 0.12 in (3 mm) wide box and place it on top of the cylinder, aligning it to the edge. Make copies of the box and place them around the cylinder to create battlements. Combine the shapes into one and make a copy of it.

12 Make a 0.79 in (20 mm) wide by 2.36 in (60 mm) tall cylinder, and place a shape from **step 11** on top. Align them and combine to make a **round tower**. Repeat the process with a taller cylinder, using the spare shape from **step 11**.

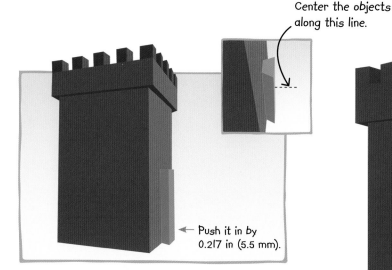

Use the align tool to center the roof and base.

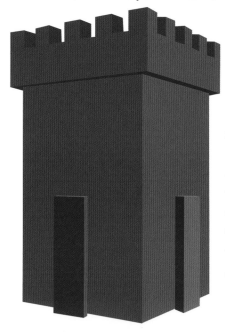

13 Now build a **square tower**. Repeat **steps 1-2**, but use the dimensions given here.

14 Take a triangle and resize it as above. Rotate it so that its sharpest corner faces the tower, and then slide it toward the tower until it just touches the wall.

Center the objects along this line.

Push it in by 0.217 in (5.5 mm).

15 Now slide the triangle into the tower by exactly 0.217 in (5.5 mm). Align the shapes so that the triangle sits in the middle of a side of the tower. Combine the shapes into one.

16 Repeat **steps 14-15**, but this time insert the triangle into an adjacent side of the tower. Combine the objects to complete your tower.

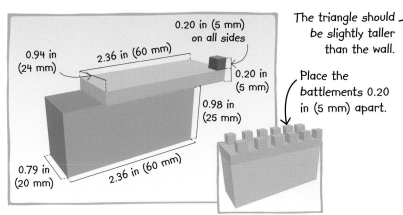

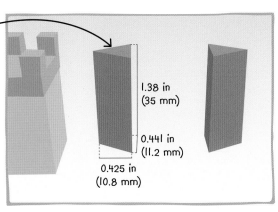

17 To make a **rampart**, take three boxes and resize and arrange them as shown above. Use the same process from **step 2** to place battlements along the top, spacing them 0.20 in (5 mm) apart. Combine the parts to make one object and then make a spare copy of it.

18 Next you'll make one of the **joints** that allow you to slot ramparts and towers together. Take a triangle and resize it as shown. Make a copy of it and flip that horizontally.

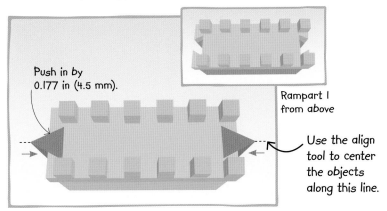

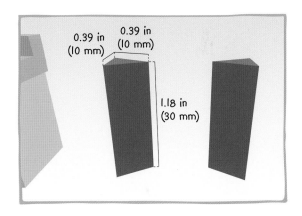

19 Place the triangles at both ends of the rampart and push each one in by exactly 0.177 in (4.5 mm). Turn the triangles into holes to complete your first rampart.

20 Take a new triangle and resize it to the dimensions shown here. Copy it and flip the copy horizontally.

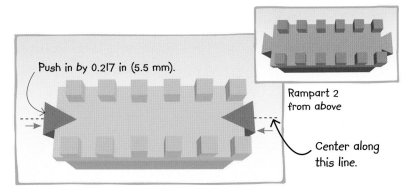

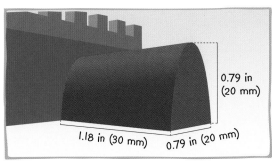

21 Place the new triangles at the either end of the spare rampart from **step 17**, with their points just touching the walls. Then push them inward by exactly 50.217 in (5.5 mm). Center them and combine. Your second rampart is now ready.

22 Make a semicircular shape, 1.18 in (30 mm) long and 0.79 in (20 mm) wide and tall. Place it next to rampart 2.

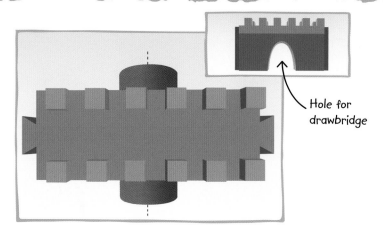

Hole for
drawbridge

23 Push the semicircular shape through the rampart so it sticks out on both sides and use the align tool to center it. Then turn it into a hole and combine. Rampart 2 now has a hole for a **drawbridge**.

24 To make the drawbridge, resize a semicircular shape and a cylinder to match the dimensions above. Rotate the cylinder by 90 degrees and place it 0.08 in (2 mm) above the work plane.

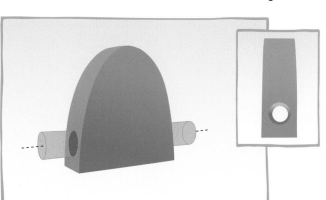

25 Pass the cylinder through the semicircular shape so that it sticks out on both sides. Align the centers of the shapes horizontally. Turn the cylinder into a hole.

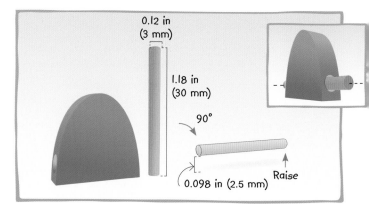

26 Resize a new cylinder to the dimensions given here. Turn it by 90 degrees and place it 0.098 in (2.5 mm) above the work plane. Pass it through the hole created in **step 25**, aligning its center with that of the hole. It should stick out of both sides evenly. Take care not to let it touch the semicircular shape at all. Combine to make your drawbridge.

Make sure there's an
even gap all the way
around the drawbridge.

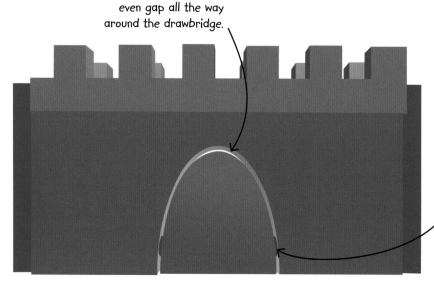

27 Place the drawbridge inside the rampart from **step 23**. Use the align tool to center it and to line it up with the front of the rampart. Zoom in to check it looks OK, then group everything together.

The combined wall and
drawbridge will print with
a working axle in place.

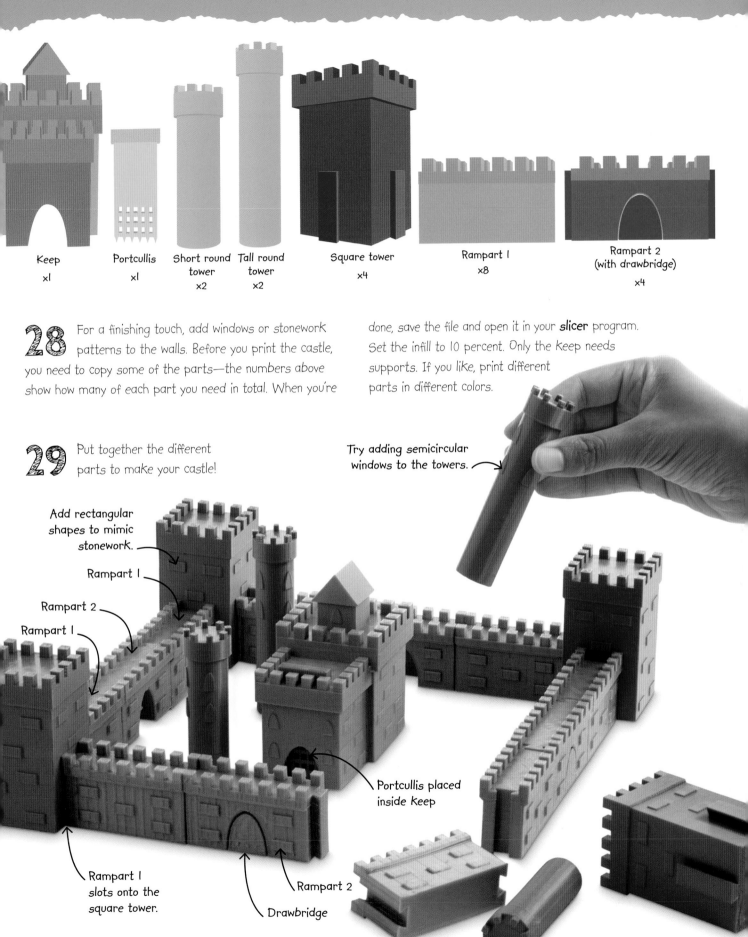

Keep
x1

Portcullis
x1

Short round
tower
x2

Tall round
tower
x2

Square tower
x4

Rampart 1
x8

Rampart 2
(with drawbridge)
x4

28 For a finishing touch, add windows or stonework patterns to the walls. Before you print the castle, you need to copy some of the parts—the numbers above show how many of each part you need in total. When you're done, save the file and open it in your **slicer** program. Set the infill to 10 percent. Only the keep needs supports. If you like, print different parts in different colors.

29 Put together the different parts to make your castle!

Try adding semicircular windows to the towers.

Add rectangular shapes to mimic stonework.

Rampart 1

Rampart 2

Rampart 1

Portcullis placed inside keep

Rampart 1 slots onto the square tower.

Rampart 2

Drawbridge

GLOSSARY

3D MODEL
A computer-generated, three-dimensional (3D) representation of an object. 3D models are used for many different things, from designing buildings to creating computer games.

3D PRINTER
A machine that creates 3D objects from digital files. Most 3D printers work by building up layers of hot, molten plastic, which hardens as it cools down.

3D SCANNING
Creating a 3D model by photographing or filming real physical objects from many different angles and combining the images on a computer.

ABS
Acrylonitrile butadiene styrene. A plastic used in some 3D printers, often for professional purposes. ABS is more durable than PLA but is less safe to use as it can produce unhealthy fumes during printing if not vented properly.

ALIGN
Arrange in a line. The align tool in a 3D modeling program is used to make separate objects line up neatly.

BITMAP GRAPHIC
A digital image made up of pixels (small dots). Digital photos are bitmap graphics. See also vector graphic.

BRIM
A wide, flat area that extends around the base of a 3D model, like the brim of a hat. Brims are added by slicer software and help models stay attached firmly to the print bed while being printed.

CAD
Computer-aided design. 3D modeling programs are often described as CAD programs.

CALIBRATION
Adjusting a printer or the software that controls a printer to make sure that the axes, print bed, and print head are all in the correct position.

DIAMETER
The width of a circle, measured along a straight line passing through the circle's center.

EXPORT
Save a file in a format that can be opened by a different kind of program.

EXTRUDER
The part of a 3D printer that melts and lays down filament.

FDM
Fused deposition modeling. The most common method used by 3D printers to print objects. FDM printers lay down material in dozens or even hundreds of thin layers, slowly building up to form a solid object.

FILAMENT
The raw material used by most 3D printers to build models. It is called filament because it is supplied as a thick thread.

GEOMETRIC MODELING PROGRAM
A 3D modeling program that creates objects from simple geometric shapes, such as cubes and spheres.

HEXAGON
A shape with six straight sides of equal length.

ILLUSTRATION
A drawing, painting, or other image that is created by hand or on a computer, rather than being captured with a camera.

IMPORT
Open a file created in a different kind of program.

INFILL
A setting used by 3D printer software to control how much hollow space there is inside an object that looks solid.

INVERT
Turn upside down.

LAYER HEIGHT
The height of the tiny layers of material laid down by a 3D printer. Setting a large layer height makes objects print more quickly, but with less fine detail.

OBJ FILE
A common file format used by 3D modeling programs and 3D printers. An OBJ file records the surface of a 3D shape as a set of geometric shapes, lines, and curves.

ORGANIC MODELING PROGRAM
A 3D modeling program that allows users to manipulate a virtual ball of clay to sculpt complex organic shapes, such as people or animals.

OVERHANG
A part of a 3D model that has no solid material directly below it. Without adequate support, an overhang may sag or collapse during printing.

PARABOLOID

A 3D shape that looks like a deep bowl.

PLA

Polylactic acid, the most common material used to make filament for 3D printers. Polylactic acid is a renewable plastic derived from corn starch and sugar cane. It is biodegradable and is also used to make biodegradable stitches. It is safe to print indoors and does not require special ventilation.

POLYGON

A shape with several straight sides. Triangles, squares, and hexagons are all types of polygon.

PRINT BED

The flat part of a 3D printer on which a model sits while it is being printed.

PRINT HEAD

The part of a 3D printer that ejects molten plastic during the printing process.

PRINT TIME

The time a 3D printer takes to print a particular object.

PRINT VOLUME

The size of the space in which a 3D printer's print head can operate. Printers with larger print volumes can print larger models.

RAFT

A wide, flat base added to a 3D model by slicer software to help stabilize while printing and provide attachment points for supports. Rafts are useful when printing models with small bases.

RESIN

A material used in SLA printers. Also called photopolymer, resin is liquid until hardened by light.

SLA

Stereolithography apparatus. A technology used by certain types of professional 3D printing machine. SLA printers use a beam of ultraviolet light or a laser to "cure" a liquid resin, turning the illuminated area solid.

SLICER PROGRAM

A program that analyzes a 3D model file and then creates a code telling a 3D printer how to output the model as a series of fine layers. Slicer programs add supports automatically and include settings to control infill and layer height.

SLM

Selective laser melting. A technology used by certain types of professional 3D printing machine. SLM printers use a powerful laser to melt and fuse metal powder, forming a solid object.

SLS

Selective laser sintering. A technology used by certain types of professional 3D printing machine. SLS printers use a laser to fuse metal or nylon powder into a solid object without fully melting it.

SPOOL

A roll of printer filament.

STL FILE

A common file format used by 3D modeling programs to save 3D models. The data in an STL file defines the surface of a 3D shape as a mesh of interconnected triangles.

SUPPORTS

Structures that prop up and stabilize a model while it is being printed. Supports are usually created by a slicer program and are printed as part of the model. They are removed by hand after printing has finished.

SVG FILE

Scalable vector graphics file. SVG is a common file format used for vector graphic files. See also vector graphic.

VECTOR GRAPHIC

A digital image made of up lines and shapes rather than pixels.

WARPING

Unwanted bending of the flat base of a model. Warping happens when a model cools quickly and isn't firmly attached to the print bed. Adding a brim can prevent it.

WORK PLANE

The flat, floorlike area in a 3D modeling program on which a model sits unless it is raised or lowered. The work plane is often represented by a colored grid.

X-AXIS

An imaginary straight line running from left to right across a graph or through a 3D space. The exact location of any point in a 3D space can be defined by saying how far along the x-, y-, and z-axes it lies. These three numbers are the point's coordinates.

Y-AXIS

An imaginary straight line running from front to back through a 3D space. The exact location of any point in a 3D space can be defined by saying how far along the x-, y-, and z-axes it lies. These three numbers are the point's coordinates.

Z-AXIS

An imaginary straight line running from top to bottom across a graph or through a 3D space. The exact location of any point in a 3D space can be defined by saying how far along the x-, y-, and z-axes it lies. These three numbers are the point's coordinates.

INDEX

ACKNOWLEDGMENTS

The publisher would like to thank the following people for their assistance in the preparation of this book:
Sam Atkinson, Bharti Bedi, Sreshtha Bhattacharya, Steven Carton, Smita Mathur, Antara Moitra, and Deeksha Saikia for editorial assistance; Mansi Agrawal, Priyanka Bansal, Rohit Bhardwaj, Neha Sharma, and Smiljka Surla for design assistance; Syed MD Farhan, Pawan Kumar, and Dheeraj Singh for illustration assistance; Nishwan Rasool for picture research assistance; Karan Bal (Data Info Source) and Gaurav Arora (Mindscape 3D Innovations) for assistance with printing 3D models; Caroline Hunt for proofreading; Elizabeth Wise for indexing; and Priscilla Nelson Cole, Abi Wright, and Kit Lane for hand modeling at photoshoots.

The publisher would like to thank the following for their kind permission to reproduce their photographs:
(Key: a-above; b-below/bottom; c-center; f-far; l-left; r-right; t-top)

4-5 iStockphoto.com: Bluehill75 (c). 4 iStockphoto.com: tonaquatic (clb). 5 Dreamstime.com: Maril408 (cb); Maril408 (cb/owl); Maril408 (crb). Instant Maker Limited (imakr): (cr). 15 Getty Images: GaryAlvis (crb). 79 Getty Images: Matej Divizna (cb); Matej Divizna (crb)

All other images © Dorling Kindersley
For further information see: www.dkimages.com